This Will Be Remembered of Her

This Will Be Remembered of Her

Stories of Women Reshaping the World

Megan McKenna

William B. Eerdmans Publishing Company

Grand Rapids, Michigan / Cambridge, U.K.

Published 2010 by
Wm. B. Eerdmans Publishing Co.
2140 Oak Industrial Drive N.E., Grand Rapids, Michigan 49505 /
P.O. Box 163, Cambridge CB3 9PU U.K.

Printed in the United States of America
www.eerdmans.com

19 18 17 16 15 14 13   7 6 5 4

Library of Congress Cataloging-in-Publication Data

McKenna, Megan.
This will be remembered of her: stories of women reshaping the world /
Megan McKenna.
p.   cm.
Includes bibliographical references.
ISBN 978-0-8028-6469-7 (pbk.: alk. paper)
1. Women and religion. 2. Women — Religious life.   I. Title.

BL458.M45   2010
230.082 — dc22

2010017327

The periwinkle, shown on the cover and inside pages of this book, is often used to symbolize the pleasures of memory.

Unless otherwise indicated, Scripture from the earlier (old) testament is from the *Jewish Study Bible: Tanakh Translation,* Jewish Publication Society, Oxford University Press, N.Y., 2004, and Scripture from the (new) Christian testament is from *The New American Bible,* St. Joseph edition, Catholic Book Publishing Co., N.Y.

DEDICATION

For Dolores, Margaret, Phyllis and Barbara,
Sandy and Barb, Maura and Maureen, Mary and Annemarie,
Patricia, and Susan, Catherine, Carol and Linda,
Mary and Grace, Betty and Vivian.

For Ying Ying, Brenda and Jo and Maybee.

For my own sisters — Cine, Mimi, Alice, Jane, and Norene —
and my mother, Marguerite, and my Nana Alice.

And for all those whose lives are a blessing and a fierce
and graceful memory for all they serve
and struggle with and love.

They say "'Anonymous' was a woman," but every woman
is known, and their names and memories are treasured
by those who share their hopes and their love
for the earth and all humankind.

Contents

Introduction

*Is God all raw nerve and we brush against such sensitivity
    in each moment — sending God quivering?
Are the beats our hearts skip a language seeking expression
    if only we'd listen?
Does the tide lick and kiss the sand and then draw back
    embarrassed to remind us how to approach each other?*

Megan McKenna, unpublished poem

We all want to be known. We all want to know. We all seek connections, intimacy, friendship, meaning, and a place on this planet where we are secure, at home. And yet we know so little without each other. Life, mystery, depths, growth, regard, love — all the crucial things that happen in the spaces between us remain unknown without another. I met a musician who both played a number of instruments and sang. I asked him, What makes the music — the notes or the spaces in between? He said it was a question he'd have to live with for a long while, something he'd have to experience and ask the music what it sensed and thought.

The poet Denise Levertov shared a most telling story. She loved to give poetry readings to sense the communication, even the communion back and forth with the audience; to listen to the silences, potent and tense; to look across a stage or a room into the eyes of strangers who became intimates as they shared their deepest places with just their presence, their attentiveness, and their eye contact.

After one such poetry reading, she thought it had gone very well. She stayed on the stage, signing books and bits of paper, chatting with people. In the midst of one conversation, two young girls no more than seventeen or eighteen came running up on stage and grabbed her. They kissed her on both cheeks, hugged her exuberantly (this was in Europe), and gushed with admiration and glee. They were at the age of discovery, discovering themselves, poetry, the universe, possibilities — everything, really. They were wild with life. She smiled, almost taken aback by their enthusiasm, and started talking with them. They were so excited — they just had to talk with her, they said.

They both were very solemn for a moment, then burst out, "We want you to know — we've found the secret to life. And we found it in one of your poems! This one line opened our eyes, our minds, and our hearts, and we will never ever be the same again — because now we know the secret to life! It will change everything we do from now on out — we know the secret!"

The girls were literally bursting with this secret! Levertov was a bit stunned and overwhelmed — the secret to life in a line of one of her poems? Amazing indeed. The girls laughed and chatted some more and then hugged her fiercely again, kissed her again on both cheeks, and jumped off the stage, running down the aisle and out the door. It all happened so fast. Their eyes were what she remembered best — they were sparkling.

And then Levertov stood on the stage — alone, though there were still many people milling around her. And suddenly she realized, *I don't know what line they're referring to — I don't even know what poem they found it in!* And she ached and longed to know where they had found it. What had they found? What was the secret? And she stood alone without the secret. And yet, she smiled and blessed them because they did find it and they did share the marvelous discovery of that treasure with her. She started to wonder, *Was it their first such discovery?* and she smiled deeper, thinking, *Oh, they have so many more secrets to life to stumble into or to find one bright morning or in the dark of night!*

Levertov was filled with gratitude — to know that she had given them, in a poem, a single line, such a gift: the secret to life! She gave the gift unknowingly, but the girls grasped hold of it and let it take them away, soaring into life. And then Levertov's heart lurched and expanded — even the horizon she thought she knew lurched too. She instinctively knew the secret because she had written a poem where it was discovered by others. The two girls found what she couldn't wrap her mind around, but now she knew it lived deep inside her — the secret to life. They would discover the secret again and again — she had lived long enough to know that — but she also remembered the first time, which sets the stage for all the other moments. *Yes, she decided, this is my life's work, my endeavor — poetry that seeks to say, 'Yes, there is a secret!'* The two girls had reminded her of that reality, that source from which came all her words, images, poems, and even the marrow of her life and relationships — the secret. There was a secret to life!

And of course, being a poet, she wrote a poem just a week after this encounter aptly entitled "The Secret." In it she describes herself: "I who don't know the/secret wrote/the line." And she's sure that when she writes this poem about the two girls, they've already forgotten the secret — so that they can discover it again "a thousand times, till death/finds them."

We need each other so much more than we realize, or remember, or take into account in our lives. Perhaps that too is a secret — one of the secrets to life: that it is primarily with others — maybe only with others — that we discover ourselves and dive into another level of our lives. Perhaps part of the secret is that it is a gift we can only give another and receive from another. There isn't really any way to find it on our own — even the two girls found the secret together.

I have tried to make this book about sharing secrets, memories, stories, and lives. Like the two young girls and the poet herself, we must assume that there is a secret and that it's not only worth sharing — it's the bedrock of our existence and the jumping-off place for our lives. Doing theology — the study of God — entails living on secrets, sifting through all the bits and pieces for the one that binds them all together. Even our world is based on a secret knowledge and awareness of gravity — what Webster's Dictionary calls "the pull of all bodies in the earth's sphere towards the earth's center." Or as monk Thomas Merton would put it: We are all one — we must remember this. Once there is that base, the other important theological issues can be tackled.

Here are some questions that perhaps need to be looked at again with new eyes, with women's eyes, with men's and women's eyes together. Who saves the tradition and incorporates contemporary technologies and knowledge? Who sees and remembers the necessary disciplines and apprenticeships and salts them with new insights and fresh wisdom — something other than the usual ideas, the acceptable or the dominant ones? Who are the masters? Who are the seanachies, the poets, the musicians, the fiddlers and dancers, the glassblowers and weavers, the knitters and healers, the medicine-keepers and the soul-keepers? Who are the street-wise theologians and preachers, the urban mystics, the mapmakers (of disintegration — of what was, what is, and how the horizons are already shifting again)? Who are the shape-shifters and the transformers — from those who convert nuclear energy to those who know how to forgive and reconcile and make lasting peace? Who are the tellers of the Word of God? Who is serious about incarnation — everybody's, since God is dwelling now in all our flesh?

Who are the mercy-givers, digging to find wellsprings of compassion that do not run dry? Who scours our hearts, succors them and breaks them wide open, stretching them to include others — more and more others? Who makes sacred space out of every landscape, alleyway, old battleground, rain forest, reclaimed and redistributed land, reservation, war-torn and destroyed region, desecrated wasteland — seeking to remind us that all ground is holy, that *here* is holy.

Who asks about our frustrations, our sexuality, our freedoms and responsibilities, our pleasures and sins, our fulfillments and losses, our loneliness and communities, our relations sterile and fertile? Who asks and tells the stories of those who hang in there, who endure, who live with grace in the midst of horror? Who tells the truth? Who knows when not to speak but to let the silence pour over us and seep into us? Who then can translate all these wisdoms and insights into every language on the face of the earth — and reclaim the ones who are lost?

Who are those who pray? Who gathers up the remnants of others' lives and relationships, holding them tenderly, healing and redeeming them? Who cries out to God on behalf of those who have no prayers, who have no one who cares for them? Who knows how to break the heart of God and call down justice when it is needed, even demanded, and mercy for those who have never known justice? Who knows how to worship, to kneel in awe, humility, and gracefulness before everyone and all creation — all the universe? Who knows how to stretch our minds and our hearts to absorb and take in, invite in all the diverse peoples of the earth? Who are the ones willing to die so that others can live? Who are the ones willing to risk it all for new wisdom, knowledge, and hope? Who knows when to break laws and ignore the rules, and when and how to make new ones that protect people, not condemn them?

And perhaps the most important ones: Who are the storytellers, who are the listeners, who are the memory-keepers of the lists and litanies of those who must be remembered? For they enflesh the theology: they take the words proclaimed and make them into the presence of their bodies, the truth of their words, and the reality of their actions. These are some of the pressing theological concerns and questions today. What are yours?

Wisdom, Story, and Truth are our sisters. And now it is time for us to give birth to their children — Compassion/Pity, Memory, and Fierceness — and to discover all around us the faces of God, whole books of revelation and bodies of life, waiting to be read and told, touched and honored. We all spend most of our lives just doing what we can — doing something good for another, standing next to someone who others shun, being a friend to someone so full of life and about to die. But it is enough. It is more than enough! It will be told of us wherever there is proclaimed the gospel of hope, of freedom and compassion, justice and mercy, truth and peace. Amen! Alleluia!

Chapter 1

This Will Be Remembered of Her

"Mercy within mercy within mercy . . ."

Thomas Merton

This book is about three closely related realities: memory, women, and resistance. Each reality is chosen for very specific and strong reasons that are found at the heart of the Gospel story in Mark of the unnamed woman who anoints Jesus' head with perfumed oil. She anoints him while he is seated at the table in the house of Simon the Leper on the outskirts of Jerusalem; it is just days before the feast of Passover. This anointing is a very intimate gesture of solidarity under tense conditions in a public setting — in the presence of Jesus' disciples and those who are just observers. This story is at the center of all these reflections. But first we need to look at the concepts and a story — a children's story based on Turkish, French, and Moroccan traditions. It has a number of names like "The Perfume of Memory" (this is a version by Michelle Nikly). I call it "What Is the Scent of Remembering?" And this is the way I tell it.

Once upon a time — it was long ago in a place most of us would consider strange and foreign, even inaccessible, and found only in tales — there was a young girl by the name of Jasime or Yasmin, her father's only child. Her mother, who was also named after that richly scented flower, had died giving birth to her. Her father, Ahmed, brought his

1

daughter up alone, but sought to live in a way that kept the memory of his beloved wife alive — and a part of their lives together. The country they dwelled in was a place of forgetfulness when this story takes place — though once it was a place filled with memories and things that can trigger memory: scents and smells. It was as though everything smelled, and fragrances pervaded the air, the land, people's clothes and hair, even objects and pieces of cloth. It had always been a marvelous place to live. Scents and smells were like a language that spoke of seasons and places, of people's work and their personalities.

The land was known for making perfumes. It was a desert with shifting sands and winds, oases of water and trees — date and nut and fig trees — and animals that could survive in the desert following faint traces of odors and were equally at home in the city. The people of the land had words for every kind of smell and scent — for the time of day and where the sun was positioned, for every adult and child, every grass and flower. They were enchanted with the natural perfumes of the place. And the most important person in the realm (besides the royal family) was the man or woman called the Master Perfume Maker. Everyone in the land worked hard at learning all the scents, the formulas, ancient and true, and making new ones. Children grew up wanting to be the Master Perfume Maker more than anything else.

But that was long ago, and things had changed. And with the changes the people forgot things — small things and much larger ones, too. Once upon a time, anyone could dream and become the Master Perfume Maker, but something had happened, and now it was only boys who could aspire to that position. And when the people forgot that everyone was equal to the task, they forgot more and more about who they really were. They forgot when certain flowers and herbs were to be reseeded or harvested. They forgot basic formulas that were essential to know before they could try mixing new scents together. And worst of all, they forgot that each scent was connected not just to its ingredients but to memories — of individuals and couples, of lovers and friends, of families, of the people and the nation and the land itself.

Ahmed hadn't forgotten that a girl child couldn't grow up to be the Master Perfume Maker. He just ignored this "tradition" and taught his daughter to sniff, smell, and breathe in deeply, to name the scents and to connect them to the ancient formulas. She began by watching how her father made the perfumes and elixirs, and then she made them exactly as he always did. When she would perfect one scent, she would bring it to her father and wait for him to inhale it deeply and listen to what he had to say: "Yes! You've captured the breeze off the sea!" or "Yes! Now you have the smell of the sand after a storm has dampened the ground!" or "Hmm . . . ah, yes! That's the smell of a peeled orange!"

But Yasmin wanted to make something new, and she had never forgotten that all the scents were connected to memories. And so she remembered all the tales and stories of her mother and the look in her father's eyes when he spoke about her, about her eyes and her hair and the way she moved in the morning. Yasmin even dreamed of what she had been like, even of her mother's dying as she gave birth to her. Then she mixed the essences together and brought the mixture to her father. He sniffed at it, inhaled it deeply, and sat down. He passed the vial under his nose again and let it sit uncorked before him. Finally he spoke: "This is not like anything I have taught you to make. It's not like anything I have ever smelled before, and yet it's so familiar, so strong, so . . . so . . ." — and then he declared it the best she had ever made! "What is it made of?" he asked.

And she told him, "I made it of freedom and grace, of hope and sacrifice, of playfulness and devotedness. I made it of your memories of mother and my hopes and desires to know her." And then they wept together.

Later that evening, Ahmed told Yasmin, "We're going to enter this in the contest where the Master Perfume Maker is chosen."

Now it had been eons since a woman had entered the contest, and the word soon spread. Finally the contest began, and after many tests and experiments, there were only two perfumes left: Yasmin's and one submitted by a man very sure of himself. It was said that he had studied with masters from all over the world. It was the Queen herself who would make the choice. She sat before all the people gathered in expectation, and she opened the man's bottle and slowly breathed in the scent — it was heavy. It was an old smell, filled with the past, with things that were strong and insistent, with things deep in the earth,

3

with mindless and forgetful sleep. It fascinated the Queen. Yasmin stood among the people and thought, *Open mine now. It's as good as any other — in fact, better! I know that it is!* And then she began to smell the scent from the open bottle. *NO!* she thought wildly. *This perfume is harsh, dangerous. The Queen can't choose that one!* But the Queen had been seduced by the scent and declared it the winner (without even touching Yasmin's glass bottle).

The Queen summoned the maker of the perfume she had chosen, and he knelt before her, head bowed and hidden in his hooded cloak. She dabbed the perfume on her wrists, in the crook of her elbows, on the sides of her neck. "What is the name of your perfume? And what is your name?" the Queen asked. But then she began to feel sick, dizzy and off-balance, and she slumped over, passing out. Still, the man stood and loudly declared, "The name of this perfume is 'Forgetfulness' or 'Oblivion' — take your pick!" And he continued, "I never forgot and I will never forget what your family did to my family: the wrongs and slights, the humiliation we endured because of what you did. You won't ever forget me, but you will forget all that is dear and cherished." And then he was gone.

The crowd gasped. The Queen was taken to bed, where she slept for days, and when she awoke, she was a very different person. She couldn't remember her name, or what country she was in, let alone that she was queen of that country. She couldn't remember her husband or her children. She couldn't remember her own childhood or favorite songs. This continued for weeks. After a while, she began sleeping very fitfully, waking from nightmares and fragments of her past. And she awakened drenched in sweat, or weeping, feeling as though she had never slept. The King sent word out to the whole realm that a reward would be given to anyone who could bring the Queen back to her senses. And Yasmin urged her father to get them an audience with the King, because she knew how to help the Queen. The arrangements were made, and when Yasmin and her father arrived for their time with the Queen, they brought boxes of scents in bottles and jars. The King wanted to know what Yasmin was going to do. Yasmin answered, "I will give the Queen back her memories and help her know who she is once again." The King wondered how she would do this.

Yasmin began by taking a vial, opening it, and passing it under the Queen's nose. "Breathe deeply — ahhh! — the smell of herbs in your favorite dish as a child. Remember the cook making it especially for you!" Yasmin did the same with a second vial. "Breathe deeply — ahhh! — it is the essence your mother wore, the scent of almonds and lemons." And a third vial: "Breathe deeply — ahhh! — it is the smell of your horse freshly lathered from a run." And a fourth vial: "Breathe deeply — ahhh! — that's the smell of the ink you know from learning to write, from signing your name, from signing your marriage bond, from recording your children's births."

And so, one after another, Yasmin gave the Queen the scents of her life and so returned her memories to her. After the healing, the Queen and the King embraced — reveling in each other's singular scent — and cried and laughed together.

And then the Queen began to make pronouncements. First she remembered that it had been ages since a girl, a woman had become the Master Perfume Maker, and she decreed that the position was open to any in the land — man or woman. Then she decreed that Yasmin was the new Master Perfume Maker. And then the King reminded her that he had promised a reward to the ones who brought the Queen back to herself. So the Queen asked Ahmed and Yasmin what they would like as a reward. They both spoke as one: "We would like you to plant bushes of jasmine everywhere in the realm so that everywhere we traveled we would remember the woman most special to us, wife and mother." And then Yasmin asked for another gift: Would the Queen appoint a Master Storyteller to record and recall all the scents and their memories and connections? That way, nothing would be lost, and the people would remember who they really were and all the amazing gifts they had been given. And so it was done. People say that the first story written down and told was this story! And a new perfume was made in honor of the ritual recovery of the memories. Now what was the name of that perfume?

This is an enchanting children's story that carries many layers of meaning. It reminds us that our memories are triggered by many things. Letters written in a familiar scrawl that we instantly recognize as coming from one we know and love. Photographs, glimpses of ourselves and others from the past, some long gone, others still with us — like bits of glass that reflect back to us what we once looked like and who we shared experiences with. Places like old houses, a favorite stretch of woods, mountains, or a lake can bring back whole seasons and repeated returns to these places. Of course, stories are reservoirs of memories — with personal, communal, and national as well as religious foundations. And our senses, especially hearing, taste, and smell, can bring memories flooding back. Music, even simple humming, can echo inside us and evoke and hold, like a bell's tone on the air, a moment from the past. With taste, the smudge on a recipe page, the licking of a spoon as batter is poured, or the hot, soft savor of homemade bread or scones puts us back at tables where we haven't sat in decades. And perhaps the strongest sense of all is that of smell, with each person having their own singular one. Cleaning polish on banisters, a cake of soap, new-mown grass, turned dirt, smoke on the edge of fall — scents are an endless litany of the past and their own storehouse of experiences.

Remember is a word that has various meanings. The Oxford Dictionary lists these: "1. keep in the memory; not forget. 2. bring back into one's thoughts. 3. convey greetings from (one person) to (another). 1. retain, keep or bear in mind; think back to. 2. recollect, think back on or to." The closely linked word *remembrance* has these meanings: "1. remembering; being remembered. 2. memory; recollection. 3. keepsake; souvenir. 4. greetings conveyed through a third person. 2. reminiscence, thought. 3. memento, reminder, token, relic. 4. regards, best wishes." Yet all these definitions might tend to lead us to think that "remembering" is primarily a function of the mind rather than of the whole body; it is an experience with external realities and features, not just personal and internal to one's awareness. To break down the word helps us understand it better. To "re-member" means to put back together the way it was; the way it is to be now; an action with intent, drawn from the past or tradition or what once was. It is a very religious word, fraught with injunctions from the Scriptures — the words of Jesus. "Do this and remember me!" In other words, "Do this (the rituals, what I did with regard to food, people, places, moments), and you will put me back together with you, with all things and all times, truthfully, wholly."

Who and what we remember is a revelation of who and what we are and hope to be. Memory carries hopes, values, wisdom, and insights. Remembering gives life beyond the grave, beyond borders, and recreates and changes history. Remembering says that repetition and imitation are important, the highest forms of respect and honor we can give to one another.

And if we join memory/remembering with women, we make a massive leap. For so many cultures, histories (even his-stories), religions, and peoples, what and who is remembered is first who won, who conquered, who survived the killing and the death, who wrote the stories and decided how the present would be remembered. So often in these stories, those who were forgotten were the women. It is said that "Women hold up half the world," but that isn't really true — women hold up more than their half. In the realm of responsibilities, they bear the lion's share. They carry the unborn for almost a year and give birth; they are the nurturers; they primarily carry the water and seed/plant/harvest and do the cooking; they are the ones who teach the fundamentals of what it means to be a human being, often while working full-time to provide for the family. More often than not, they do this without clean water, basic health care, or education, while in a land that is affected by violent weather and natural disasters, and where violence, war, and aggression lead to a dearth of basic necessities, lost homes, and lost countries. And often their own persons and bodies are seen as part of what is easily and quickly sacrificed, fodder for enemies — for raping, maiming, kidnapping, honor killings, torture, and brutality. Women are treated as possessions, as barter, as something to be used, punished, and humiliated — as less than human, given even poorer treatment than animals.

In many circles of literature, art, and even science there is a saying: "'Anonymous' was a woman." Women are more easily and more quickly forgotten, both singularly and together — with the added stigmas of religious, sociological, racial, and cultural prejudices. It is worth noting that in the Gospels Jesus defends, protects, stands with, and praises women in public. He insists often (as we will see) that his disciples — the twelve male ones — observe and imitate the women he relates to and holds up as examples of what true disciples do and are.

In most cases, the men ignore his words for the moment — but oddly enough, the women are remembered and their stories are told in the Scriptures!

The story that sets the foundation for this book is found in the first account of the good news: the Gospel of Mark. It is the last story — one so fraught with power and wisdom — before Jesus goes into Jerusalem to be sentenced to death. It is his last public appearance, his last moment to teach. The story is told and experienced in a climate of conspiracy, tension, violence, and religious fervor as well as political intrigue and collusion among members of his own following, the leaders of the people, and their military governor and occupying Roman army. This is the story, with the short introduction that reminds us of what's going on in the city, followed by the actual moment of encounter, and ending with the reconnection back to the larger picture:

The Passover and the Feast of the Unleavened Bread were to take place in two days' time. So the chief priests and the scribes were seeking a way to arrest him by treachery and put him to death. They said, "Not during the festival, for fear that there may be a riot among the people."

When he was in Bethany reclining at table in the house of Simon the leper, a woman came with an alabaster jar of perfumed oil, costly genuine spikenard. She broke the alabaster jar and poured it on his head. There were some who were indignant. "Why has there been this waste of perfumed oil? It could have been sold for more than three hundred days' wages and the money given to the poor." They were infuriated with her. Jesus said, "Let her alone. Why do you make trouble for her? She has done a good thing for me. The poor you will always have with you, and whenever you wish you can do good to them, but you will not always have me. She has done what she could. She has anticipated anointing my body for burial. Amen, I say to you, wherever the gospel is proclaimed to the whole world, what she has done will be told in memory of her."

Then Judas Iscariot, one of the Twelve, went off to the chief priests to hand him over to them. When they heard him they were pleased and promised to pay him money. Then he looked for an opportunity to hand him over. (Mark 14:1-11)

There are other stories of Jesus being anointed — usually his feet are anointed — and they are not to be confused with this first account, so closely associated with Jesus' fast-approaching torture, crucifixion, and death. The story is told within the religious context of the Feast of the Unleavened Bread — the Passover, remembering the exodus to freedom from Egypt, the place of bondage and slavery. It is a meal in Simon the leper's house (though he must be cured, because no one would approach or enter his house if he were still ritually and physically unclean). And the meal that is cited as the future reality for all forever is the meal originally taken in haste by the Israelites. They stood and ate together of the lamb, the bitter herbs, and the unleavened bread — the meal of freedom, the meal of hope, the meal that reveals the future of a people that live not in slavery but in a promised land of justice and peace for all. So all those gathered at Simon's house are reclining at table. Think of three long tables with enough room between them that servants could come and go on both sides with food and drink. The guests recline with their feet away from the table.

Outside the house, in Bethany, a suburb of Jerusalem, the night is filled with meetings of clandestine groups, and ugly plots of treachery and conspiracy of how to arrest and murder an innocent man. Those who are intent on killing Jesus are aware that he means a great deal to the people — he is their hope of a prophet, a savior, a messiah. In the tradition of Moses, he is the liberator and the law-giver; he is the one that the other prophets promised — the one who would be the presence of hope personified. So for the plotters, timing is crucial; they must pull off this evil deed without triggering a riot. The memory of Passover is strong — its emphasis on freedom and justice, even for slaves — so they must be doubly careful.

Inside Simon's house, Jesus and his disciples and Simon and his friends are dining. Sometime during the course of the meal — after the first course, after the main dishes, or at the end, near dessert — a woman comes in. She is not described at all — they are interested only in what she is carrying. It is an alabaster jar of perfumed oil, pure spikenard worth 300 days' wages — a year's worth of work. This jar and its contents are extravagant, outlandishly so. The woman goes straight to Jesus, breaks open the jar, and pours its contents on his head. She would be standing beside him, with him lying on the divan, the top of his head at her waist. Did she break the alabaster jar on the table, the floor? It was probably like a perfume bottle, about 6-10 inches high, and held a few ounces. Once she had poured the oil on his head (in absolutely shocked silence, most likely), the oil would have run down his hair and down his face and through his beard, dripping eventually onto the tablecloth. It would only have taken a few moments. And then, it seems, all hell breaks loose.

People are indignant. Their emotions escalate in intensity and power. They don't talk about her! They're concerned about the costliness of the jar and its contents and its utter waste — according to them. It is a blunt insult to Jesus — wasted on him! And then they try to cover their rage with a religious or moral reason: the oil could have been sold and the money given to the poor! One is wont to ask, When was the last time that they, or any of us — or anyone, for that matter — "wasted" a year's wages on the poor? The people's feelings have now gone up a decibel to infuriation, to rage and anger barely controlled.

And then Jesus responds, and he too talks not to the woman but about her. But he aligns himself with her, taking her place, her defense, in solidarity and attentiveness to her, her gesture of great respect, her act of honoring and her presence so close to him. He is blunt: "Leave off, back off; don't make trouble for her. She's with me, attending me with goodness." Everyone in the room had witnessed her act of ritual anointing, and they knew that anointing someone's head with oil was reserved for kings, priests, prophets, and those in authority. Jesus lets her action stand — it is appropriate and due to him.

And then he tackles their religious blaming of the woman by associating himself with the poor. They can take a year's wages whenever they wish — every year, every other year, every third year — and give it to the poor, but she has singled him out as poor now, and here in this place, at this moment. And he clearly and publicly says that she has done what she could under the circumstances — which everyone else is aware of but ignoring: that she has anointed his body for burial

10

now, anticipating that the moment will soon come when he will be dead. He is about as clear as he can be: "The poor you will always have with you, and whenever you wish you can do good to them, but you will not always have me." There are two things worth noting in this three-part sentence. The first is that the reality of the poor is with us always — it's a fact, not what is meant to be, or should be. The poor are with us because we do not share enough and we do not give enough, and so the divide, the gap remains. And whenever we wish, we can do good. This kind of giving is based more on our desires than on their needs — which are constant and demanding always. The second thing worth noting is "you will not always have me." Historically, it seems, this last part of the sentence has been the most problematic. It has been used to justify all sorts of things that have to do with building churches — and all the ornate, expensive vessels and materials in those churches — while ignoring the poor.

Jesus' saying "You will not always have me" is his stating a fact that he is trying to make his followers face: he will not be with them always — in fact, he is going to be dead within a few days' time. The woman has sensed this reality and read what is going on all around them and has decided to stand in public with him. His followers are ignoring what is swirling around them and concentrating on details that are meaningless in the larger picture of what is happening to him. The woman has done a corporal work of mercy — the most highly valued one in the Jewish community. She has prepared his body for burial (as the women will attempt to do after the crucifixion, the burial, and the passing of the Sabbath vigil), and she has anointed the body of a criminal, a criminal who is to be crucified. This act of mercy is what she could do — it is her public act of honor, of acknowledging who he is, of aligning herself with him, with his teaching and his person. She offers her physical presence and her tenderness and, in her way, an act of resistance to what will be done to his body: it will be sacrificed by those authorities intent on making a point and retaining their power base. Hers is an act of resistance born of mercy. It is a touch of mercy, yet she never actually touches him, only pours the perfumed oil over his head, releasing the strong, distinct smell of spikenard. For the moment she knows delicious anonymity. And she disappears into Jesus' mind and heart. It is profligate mercy. It is the beginning of a movement: how to resist with mercy.

But Jesus is also saying, "She is doing this for me now/here. If you want to do this for me, my own body won't always be here, but the poor will always be here with you, and I will be with them. Whatever you want to do for me, please, do it for them, and I will take it that you did it for me." The woman has understood his teaching that God is with us in the flesh and blood of Jesus and with us in the flesh and blood, the bodies of all, especially the broken ones, the broken body of Christ, still crucified, still in need of honoring with corporal works of mercy, of tender regard, of allegiance and alliance, of resistance to what is happening all around and causing this pain, suffering, and death in the first place.

But then comes the line which does not appear anywhere else in the Gospel, a proclamation reserved for this woman: "Amen, I say to you, wherever the gospel is proclaimed to the whole world, what she has done will be told in memory of her" (Mark 14:9). Other translations read, "what she has done will be told in remembrance of her," or simply, "This will be remembered of her." This is to be an integral part of the proclamation of the gospel for all times and all places! This memory is an intimate part of Jesus' own memory and our remembrance of his living, suffering, dying, being prepared for burial, and rising again. This is a necessity that must be included in all our preaching and teaching and proclamation of the Scriptures. And that is what this book is about: remembering women who act in public even within intimate settings, honoring the despised and those about to suffer and be executed, tortured and maimed, killed for religious, political, and national reasons — aligning themselves with anyone pushed to the edge, seen as the enemy, treated as less than human, who is poor here, now, in every place among every group of religious people.

The intent of this book is to acknowledge and raise up women past and contemporaneous, in every culture and religion, on every geographical continent, who make even one gesture in public (perhaps repeated many times), who perform a corporal work of mercy that associates them with criminals, with the dying and those that others conspire against, intending to arrest them and kill them with no concern for their persons. It is to remember women who resist the evil around them with gestures of tenderness and honor, who stand with those in vulnerable positions and places, who are prophetic because they stand next to those pushed to the edges, to the brink. They may not ever say a word, but their intentions and actions are clear: they are witnesses to humanity, for humankind, and they use all their resources to say where they stand and who they are with — in spite of danger and rejection from within their own communities, even within their own religious groups, as well as within the larger context of armies, nations, and political adversaries of those they approach with such care and closeness. This book is about those women who break with the respectable, the influential, the institutional and dominant, those in charge, even with the inner circles of the world. They read the prevailing winds of economics, politics, religion, and culture and smell the air of death, of manipulation and control, of abuse of power and lack of humanity, while smelling too the fear and insecurity, the pain, the cries and the silence of those who are victims and treated inhumanely.

The story in Mark goes on, sadly enough. Judas Iscariot, named and described as one of the Twelve, part of Jesus' intimate group of followers, leaves after the anointing and tells those intent on killing Jesus that he will "hand him over to them" — a brutal phrase of callousness which reveals that he is with them, not with Jesus. And there is money involved again. While the woman "wasted" a year's worth of wages, we learn later that Judas is willing to sell Jesus for just thirty pieces of silver — a paltry amount. What is a human being's life worth? What she is willing to spend in money, resources, presence, touch, time, public association, and future ramifications, or what he's willing to chance — and his life shifts with the intent to look for an opportunity to destroy, while her life seizes on the opportunity to heal, to help, to redeem and make more human in horrific circumstances. She is grace under fire and a shaft of light and hope in the midst of terror and rejection.

This story reminds us that we must be prepared and that we must never underestimate the power and force of hate and what human beings can inflict on one another's bodies and souls, even daring to give

13

religious reasons for the horror that will be inflicted. We cannot be naïve or stupid — retaliation and punishment will likely be part of the stand we take. The woman shares Jesus' courage, his terror and sadness, his loneliness and his faithfulness as he nears the time of betrayal, rejection, torture, and death. What are we to remember as gospel?

She is to be remembered. Her story is to be told. Judas is named. Simon the leper is named. Jesus is named. And her — what is her name? Generally in the past she has had no name. But the Gospel writers have quirks that one has to learn to read, and it turns out that she does have a name. After all, if you're going to be remembered for one thing that you do — and it is to be proclaimed throughout all time and throughout the whole world — it can't just be "her." Because this has been the case for so so many who are worth remembering and telling the story of — or who are known only to those locally or those who were touched with tender regard and the resistance of mercy and gracefulness. (There will be a chapter on those unnamed women, and we will meet this woman again.)

Just two chapters after the story of the anointing — after Jesus has been rejected, handed over, tortured, scourged, driven to the hill of execution, his arms bound as a slave's to a cross bar, and then hung on wood until he died and was hastily dropped into a grave provided by another — there is the rest of the story. It is in Mark 16:1-8, which is the original ending of the Gospel. And it begins this way:

> When the Sabbath was over, Mary Magdalene, Mary, the mother of James, and Salome bought spices so that they might go and anoint him. . . .

These are the first of eight women — called in the Eastern churches "the myrrh-bearing women" — who are named: Mary of Magdala, who appears in all of the accounts of the Resurrection; Mary, the mother of James (in some manuscripts "James the Less" — one of the disciples); and Salome. This last woman is only mentioned once in this Gospel, and she appears nowhere else. She is remembered for one deed, one act of solidarity, a corporal work of mercy, an intent to do good for another that will put her in danger, a determination to say

14

with her presence that she believed and she stood with Jesus — and wherever the gospel is preached in all the world, Salome is remembered. She is the last named figure of Mark's Gospel! (The rest of the chapter is a number of add-ons after the original testimony.) And she is seen in her community with other women who with courage, perhaps even with desperate devotion, continue to be human in the face of horror, violence, and vicious destruction of other human beings. And it is these women who set in motion the power of the Resurrection. Her name is Salome.

And so, if each of us was to be remembered for just one deed, one gesture of human touch, for one corporal work of mercy, alone or with others, an act that put us in association with one or some of "them" deemed criminal or simply expendable by others, an act of resistance in doing good for another, or in resisting violence and collusion by saying silently with touch and presence NO to hatred, killing, suffering laid on others, the cross, and deprivation — and all of it often connected to economics and money, power and the military, those in control, not serving the people's needs for hope — what would that gesture, that act, be? If we were to be remembered by a gesture of resistance, a moment of mercy, what would it be — what would we do?

This book will look at Gospel stories and the stories of children and traditions around the world, but specifically at women, real women, still alive and kicking and working in resistance, tenderness, and justice. And this book will look prophetically at those in our traditions, in all religions and countries, and "they will be remembered" for their decision to be the good news in their place and their time.

And you — if you were to be remembered for just one gesture, one act of solidarity, one touch of kindness, one prophetic stance, one bit of human hope, one moment of mercy — what would you want to be remembered for?

Chapter 2

Women of Water and Women of Words

Three children on the riverbank. A pair of twins and another, whose mauve corduroy pinafore said Holiday! in a tilting, happy font.

Wet leaves in the trees shimmered like beaten metal. Dense lumps of yellow bamboo dropped into the river as though grieving in advance for what they knew was going to happen. The river itself was dark and quiet. An absence rather than a presence, betraying no sign of how high and strong it really was.

Arundhati Roy, *The God of Small Things: A Novel*

Water and words and women: they are a formidable and fundamental trinity, seamlessly braided together through life, through history, and through survival and communication — existence itself. As the quotation above suggests, water is a constant presence in our lives — it's just there. In First World countries we often take it for granted, but for most women and men, the necessity of water for continued health, growth, sustenance, and life itself is increasingly in the forefront of their minds because of the stark scarcity of its existence.

Strange that on a planet where four-fifths of its circumference is covered with water, most of us are thirsty! But in the past only about 6 percent of that water was drinkable. Now, because of climate change and humankind's interference and pollution, only about 2 to 3 percent of it is drinkable, and a good deal of that is in the form of ice. Frighteningly enough, only .007 percent of all the water on earth is available to drink. And we are thirsty for good reason: our bodies are made up primarily of water! Statistics say that 60 percent of our body is water, 70 percent of our brain is water, and 80 percent of our blood is water. Most of us wouldn't last longer than a week without water. Scientists try to keep reminding us that all life on earth emerged from the waters of our world. Even our Judeo-Christian heritage in writing begins with these familiar words:

Bereshit

When God began to create heaven and earth — the earth being unformed and void, with darkness over the surface of the deep and a wind from God sweeping over the water — God said, "Let there be light"; and there was light. (Genesis 1:1-3a)

The very "stuff" that the Holy One uses to begin the process of creating is water, darkness/deep, wind and words. We live thirsty — for water, for life, for God, for words, for all that is fundamental to life, to living as human beings. Every religion begins its creation stories with water, sensing from its beginnings that our existence and presence upon the earth depend on water. We speak of earth, air, fire, and water as the elements of all life. In Asia there are five elements: earth, air, fire, water, and wood. In Hinduism the elements are earth, air, fire, water, and space. For most indigenous peoples, we are all birthed in waters. Even today, many women who are about to have a baby find fresh running water, then go into the water and give birth, mixing the water of their wombs with the water of the earth mother as sky father hovers protectively. In China, the laws of the universe are bound closely to the laws of morality, values, and the laws of relationship among human beings. In the Tao, water is the primary source, flow, and transformative teaching symbol for all who dwell in the world.

The religions of the Book (words) begin and end with water in Genesis and Revelation, and we will look at some of the innumerable stories of Judaism and Christianity. In Islam, Allah is the creator of water, and all creatures came forth from water. Dr. Gary Chamberlain writes,

According to the Qur'an, "Allah has created from water every living creature." Water is a symbol of Paradise, a reminder of Allah's gift in a harsh, desert climate. Wells are especially venerated because of water's scarcity. Muslim laws view water as a communal resource. A hierarchy exists among uses: first, the right of thirst, i.e., no one can be denied drinking water since life is involved; then needs of bathing, cleaning, and cooking; next, livestock; and lastly, irrigation of crops. The very purpose of water is to revive the earth and all upon it.[1]

Water — ancient stories tell of this precious gift and how we are connected to it, how we are to use it and treasure it, even how we got it in the beginning. It is always the animals who secured the water first — and shared it with humans. And the stories always describe it as a struggle, a quest, a journey into the unknown — the depths — swimming through the dark, murky salt waters to find fresh, sweet drinking water.

The people of the tribes/clans are always mindful of their interdependence with the earth and its resources as well as their close proximity to the animals, birds, fish, and all other living creatures that share these resources with them. The water they need isn't just any water on the face of the earth — it has to be spring-fed water, fresh-running, flowing water. Those that find water and seek to bring it back to the others have to taste it first to see if it is drinkable. And it is always a small, insignificant creature that in the end secures the water — a snail (the snail's silvery trail), a spider (the spider's clay pot), or a turtle (the turtle's shell). And in many of the stories about water, it is Snail Girl, Spider Woman, or Mother Turtle who makes the perilous and exhausting journey to bring the gift back to the people and all creation.

The Navajo have a saying: "Where water is scarce, there is truth." They know and remember that the earth's water supply is not infinite and that it must be protected, cherished, and appreciated.

Our need for water daily for our health and well-being, for normal growth, cannot be ignored. Today the world is experiencing a major universal water crisis. One in three people lack access to adequate sanitation; one in five do not have access to safe drinking water; a child dies every fifteen seconds from a water-related disease. In 2008, twenty-five million refugees were displaced by contaminated rivers — that's more people than were forced to flee from war zones.[2]

There is a short but profound story told in Africa — from Kambaland in Kenya — that reminds us of the connections between water, human beings, survival, and devotion or religion.

Once upon a time, there was a land with many water wells. Over the years many had been found to be natural rainwater caches, and many more had been dug by the people as they migrated across the parched land so that both humans and animals would have water on their journeys. A few were fed by underground springs, but most were filled with rainwater. It was a hard time when the rains did not come and the well water was low. It was during one of these times that an old woman came upon a young girl sitting by a well on the outskirts of the village. "What are you doing here?" the woman asked. "Are you thinking? Are you thirsty?"

The girl looked up at her and said, "I am waiting for the rains to come again to fill the well so that I might drink again."

The old woman shook her head and said, "You will be here a long time, child. During these months of the year, you must kneel on the earth, grasp hold of the edge of the well, and bend your head down to drink. The wells are shallow, so you must learn to kneel to slake your thirst."

So simple — learn to kneel and drink. It should be our attitude toward the waters of the earth always — to live with reverence and awareness. This notion of devotion and water being a source of wisdom, knowledge, and grace that sustains the inner world as well as our bodies is found throughout all religious and cultural traditions. There is a story told in Brazil — nearly the same story told by Buddhist masters — of one who wants to be taught wisdom and learn how to find it and extract it from life and the earth. This is how I tell the story from Brazil, from the area around Santa Cruz, where people depend primarily on rainwater to keep the rivers and streams filled.

Once upon a time there was a young man who lived in a village. He was a good hunter, a man careful of others and kind to those in need. He would share what he caught with young and old and would work

19

in the fields with the women to help them with the planting and harvesting. His name was Ramon, and when he saw the lovely and graceful young woman Inez, he wanted to ask her to marry him. Finally he approached her and asked the question. And he was taken aback by her answer: "No — I can't marry you. I'm sorry. You see, I know that you are strong, that you are careful of others and share with them, but I could never marry someone who wasn't wise as well."

Ramon was momentarily stunned speechless. And then he responded, "I will do anything you ask. I will learn wisdom!" But then he was without words again — how, where would he find wisdom?

Inez smiled at him. "Good. I know just the person who can help you. Go downriver for three days and three nights, and you will find a campsite and the old one, Ignacio. He can teach you. And when you have wisdom, come back and ask me again."

The young man lost no time and left early the next morning. Three days and three nights later, he pulled his canoe onto the shore, where he found an old man with smiling eyes waiting for him. Ramon poured out his heart to Ignacio, begging him to teach him wisdom, telling him that he would do anything to be able to marry Inez. "Good," the old man said. "Let's get started right away with your first lesson. We can begin right here, near the water's edge." And he waded into the water a foot or two. "Come," he invited Ramon. "Kneel in the waters and get a closer look."

Ramon waded in and knelt and bent his head down to look. And without warning the old man pushed his head down into the water. For an old man, he was good and strong. He held Ramon's head under — while he squirmed, trying to come up for air, and swallowed water. It seemed like ages before Ignacio let him up — spitting, indignant, his composure utterly gone. When he could talk again, Ramon blurted out, "You tried to drown me!"

The old man looked at him soberly and asked, "What were you thinking about when your head was under water?"

And Ramon blurted out: "Air!"

The old man continued, "Were you thinking about how good you are at hunting and helping others?"

"No!" Ramon gagged and said again, "Air!"

And the questions kept coming: "Were you thinking about her?"

"No!" Ramon yelled at him. "Air! Just air!"

"Well," said Ignacio, "you have finished your first lesson."

Ramon sat in the water, drenched and bedraggled. "I don't understand."

Ignacio looked at him and said, "When you want wisdom as much as you want air under water — you'll find that you have wisdom!"

Poor Ramon! He nearly started to cry. "Then I never will marry Inez!" "Well," Ignacio said, "I guess you should go back and tell her." And he turned and went back onto the shore and disappeared into the jungle, leaving Ramon sitting in the shallows.

Ramon got up and got back into his canoe. And it was a longer trip back than three days and three nights. How could he face Inez and tell her what had happened and that he would never have the wisdom she required to marry him? Finally he came back to the village, and it was Inez who found him and drew him aside on the path, eager to find out if he had gotten wisdom so that she could marry him. "Are you wise? Did you get wisdom from Ignacio?"

And Ramon was quiet at first, trying to find the right words; the truth was hard to speak. "No, my beloved Inez, I am not wise, and I probably never will be."

"But what did Ignacio teach you?" Inez asked.

Ramon's head was bowed; he just couldn't look her in the eye. "He taught me the first lesson only: that when I want wisdom as much as I want air when my head is under water, then I will be wise. I think I was supposed to learn that water and air are more important than wisdom."

And surprisingly, Inez was delighted. "Well," she said, "since you have come this far, I'll marry you."

Again, Ramon couldn't speak at first; it took time for her words to seep into his mind and his heart. "I don't understand!" he exclaimed. "I'll be an ancient before I'm wise!"

And Inez looked at him with great tenderness and love. "I know, but that's all right. You have learned much about wisdom, and I have learned that you speak the truth no matter what, and that you are humble and close enough to the earth and air and water to live with their wisdom. You are willing to do anything to find wisdom, and you love me. Come, let us learn together how to be wise — and perhaps we can begin by returning to Ignacio and doing the second lesson together!"

And so it was, they say. And these two — Inez and Ramon — were known in many villages along the river for both their love and their wisdom.

This wisdom tale comes from South America, but it is universal in its method, its telling, and its insights. Wisdom. It is the first attribute of God in many religions; it is the first gift given when Christians are baptized and confirmed; it is the depth of understanding and awareness that is as vast as the oceans binding us truthfully to all of creation, the world, and God.

One of the most loved and prayed psalms of David is Psalm 63. Its lines are familiar to many.

A Psalm of David, when he was in the Wilderness of Judah
God, You are my God;
    I search for You,
    my soul thirsts for You,
    my body yearns for You,
    as a parched and thirsty land that has no water.
I shall behold You in the sanctuary,
    and see Your might and glory.
Truly Your faithfulness is better than life;
    my lips declare Your praise.
I bless You all my life;
    I lift up my hands, invoking Your name.
I am sated as with a "rich feast,"
    I sing praises with joyful lips
    when I call You to mind upon my bed,
    when I think of You in the watches of the night;
    for You are my help,
    and in the shadow of Your wings
    I shout for joy.
My soul is attached to You;
    Your right hand supports me. (vv. 1-9)

This is a prayer that is universal — the thirst for the Holy, for mystery, for wisdom and understanding, for intimacy and connection to The Other. This is desire, longing from deep within, a desperate need, and it is expressed externally by extending and raising arms and hands upward (a universal prayer position). Our souls are like deserts, parched and sere lands, desperately needing rain; our spirits are gasping for air underwater. Our words reveal the deepest recesses of what it means to be human — to mystically seize hold of all things made, learning wisdom from them; and to be seized by the One who is the maker, keeper, and holder of all things, a revelation in all that surrounds us. We are "attached" to the Holy One, and we live in the shadow of the wings of God. The air we breathe, the waters we drink — all earth is our sanctuary.

These images of water, of rain, of thirst seep through the books of the Bible, from Genesis through Exodus and the prophets. The book of Zechariah (Nevi'im) is concerned with restoring the people, through repentance, to God; rebuilding the temple where they can worship Yahweh together; and the people's living bound to the words of covenant and the prophet's exhortations. And there are many references of hope, seeding the promises of a messianic time of abiding justice and deep-seated peace. Zechariah is a book full of visions and flying scrolls and words about liturgy, but it is also filled with everyday realities: of rain and water overlapping with the presence and mystery of God dwelling with the people, who belong to the Holy One. The people are told,

> Ask the Lord for rain
> in the season of late rain.
> It is the Lord who causes storms;
> And He will provide rainstorms for them,
> grass in the fields for everyone. (Zechariah 10:1)

And in the last chapter of the prophet's exhortations, the people are told what is coming: "In that day, fresh water shall flow from Jerusalem, part of it to the Eastern Sea and part to the Western Sea, throughout the summer and winter. And the Lord shall be king over all the earth; in that day there shall be one LORD with one name" (Zech. 14:8-9). It was during this time that in Jerusalem massive amounts of water would be released from the temple into the streets of the city — a glimpse of Zechariah's vision for all the people to see as they stood in the water. The translation of "fresh water" is also "living water," and this is a phrase that Jesus uses often, not only in the temple environs but also in foreign regions like Samaria in the desert's noonday heat.

The ancient story of the woman of Samaria coming to draw water and encountering Jesus' presence is steeped in all these overlapping symbols of living water, wells, the need for water to sustain daily life, the undercurrents of waters of life and mystical knowledge, wisdom and words of truth that lead to a richer and deeper life. Here is the first part of the story, where Jesus and the woman meet and talk of waters.

Now when Jesus learned that the Pharisees had heard that Jesus was making and baptizing more disciples than John (although Jesus himself was not baptizing, just his disciples), he left Judea and returned to Galilee.

He had to pass through Samaria. So he came to a town of Samaria called Sychar, near the plot of land that Jacob had given to his son Joseph. Jacob's well was there. Jesus, tired from his journey, sat down there at the well. It was about noon.

A woman of Samaria came to draw water. Jesus said to her, "Give me a drink." His disciples had gone into the town to buy food. The Samaritan woman said to him, "How can you, a Jew, ask me, a Samaritan woman, for a drink?" (For Jews use nothing in common with Samaritans.) Jesus answered and said to her, "If you knew the gift of God and who is saying to you, 'Give me a drink,' you would have asked him and he would have given you living water." [The woman] said to him, "Sir, you do not even have a bucket and the cistern is deep; where then can you get this living water? Are you greater than our father Jacob, who gave us this cistern and drank from it himself with his children and his flocks?"

Jesus answered and said to her, "Everyone who drinks this water will be thirsty again, but whoever drinks the water I shall give will never thirst; the water I shall give will become in him a spring of water welling up to eternal life." The woman said to him, "Sir, give me this water, so that I may not be thirsty or have to keep coming here to draw water." (John 4:1-15)

It is said that overfamiliarity can breed contempt. Whether or not that is true, overfamiliarity can certainly muddy the waters and keep us from seeing, hearing, and understanding — catching the wisdom of the words of a piece of Scripture. The obvious sometimes needs to be stated.

It is the middle of the desert and the middle of the day — the hottest, driest, most sere time when thirst is strongest. Jesus is thirsty from his journey, exhausted, and finds himself in Samaria — a part of the land that split from Jerusalem hundreds of years before. The Jerusalem people and the Samarian people mutually despise each other, each considering the other to be traitors, heretics, and sinners in every regard: theologically, religiously, liturgically, politically (in regards to Roman occupation), economically, socially, and so forth. This is the reason for the blatant hostility that the woman exhibits when Jesus demands that she give him a drink — from her source of water.

The backdrop is the theological question of baptism. John the Baptizer's baptism was one of repentance that would lead to the forgiveness of sins. We are told that Jesus doesn't baptize, that only his disciples do. This catapults us into the time of the Gospel's writing — probably around the late nineties, more than sixty years after the resurrection of Jesus, when baptism was the initiation into the community, the illumination of the mysteries of faith, and the confirmation of the believer's commitment to the Body of Christ, inviting the baptized one into the sharing of the feast of Eucharist and Word. And historically it helps to know that the first group of people who in large numbers became part of the Christian community — specifically, the community of the Beloved Disciple, the community of the Gospel of John — were, in fact, the Samaritans, who had been the enemies of the Jews during the lifetime of Jesus. The story takes place in a physical desert, but it is also a desert of hate, distrust, and enemies. And it is Jesus who initiates the conversation, the encounter, and the ritual of gift-giving and sharing water.

We are given lots of theological history — geographical places bound to the ancestors of Jacob and Joseph, the tradition of belief separated from the Jews' ancestor in faith: Abraham. She is covenanted to Yahweh through a different line of faith and belief, though the Samaritans still considered themselves part of the covenant. The Jews, however, considered them heretics, outside the covenant, betrayers of belief because of their accommodation to the gods/idols of those who conquered them after the Northern and Southern Kingdoms split. They had been overrun and subjugated by five nations and now lived under the shadow of the Roman army and governor, but they had made deals and contracts with each succeeding nation so that they could both practice their own rituals and religion as well as worship the idols of those who invaded them. The Romans afforded them economic and political stability, and the Romans did not see them as enemies but more as trading partners, people to be dealt with more diplomatically than the accursed Jews.

This is the face-to-face, unexpected encounter of two enemies on many levels: political, economic, cultural, and religious — to say nothing of gender. It begins with spitfire words and emotions close to the surface. Jesus is first: "Give me a drink." It is a demand, not a courteous asking. And the woman spits back, basically saying, "Who do you think you are to demand water from me — a Samaritan and also a woman?" She is stating the obvious in case he hasn't noticed where he is. He is outside Israel and in her region now, and he has forgotten who he is — a Jew whose culture and laws forbade interaction with those who were heretic and unclean. Jesus doesn't help things along with his response. He basically tells her, *"I'm God's gift to you — if you only knew."* In reply to the first demand, most people even today would say, "You want a drink? Get it yourself. Or at least say 'please.'" And now to be told that this total stranger is the gift of God for you — most people wouldn't think so.

But now the conversation and banter back and forth takes off, and there are levels of meaning, innuendo, and symbols all swirling together. For the Jews as well as the Samaritans, there were double meanings for the phrase "living water." First is the common meaning still held today around the world: living water is fresh water from deep in the earth that is always seeking a way up and out. Jesus is sitting at the well that is filled with living water — which has been there for more than three thousand years at the time he is there with her — from Jacob and Joseph's time. And the well is still there: it is the primary source of fresh drinking water for the entire West Bank of Palestine in the city of Nablus. It is the source, the center of life, of survival, of commerce; it is the heart of the city, even now. The Israelis have sought on many occasions to bomb the well, to poison it and divert it so that there would be no internal source of water for the Palestinians and they would have to rely on the Israelis even more — just to survive daily in the desert. Living water can be blocked or dammed, but when it is stopped from flowing up and outward — by stones, mesh, debris, and so on — it simply goes back down into the earth more deeply, goes around the obstacle, and then comes back up again, seeking release. When I have stayed with people in southeast Asia, they were often waiting for the douser to arrive and do his work: find caches of living water on their land.

But the other meaning of "living water" is just as common in Judaism, Christianity, and Islam: Living water is a drink of the Torah, the Scriptures, the Word of God. And so Jesus will begin to use the phrase not only to speak about the water in the well beside him but also to speak about the water of the Word of God. It is a code word with a tag of long history, and the woman catches it immediately and speaks to him with more respect, calling him "sir." And when he says he has something to give her — a drink of living water — she's interested, and she begins to talk theology to him. She goes back to her tradition of Jacob and Joseph and mentions her long heritage that is active even up to her day and time. And she throws in — slipping back into the other meaning — that the well is deep (both in richness of religious meaning and in physical proximity that is so near and yet so far away), and he is without a bucket or a way to get to the water. Now they are engaged both religiously as well as physically, needing water in the desert in the noonday heat. She reminds him that this water and her tradition have sustained her people over thousands of years, and that she has the bucket to dip down into it.

Jesus does not contradict her words, but pulls her further along into the discussion, saying, "If you drink this water, you will be thirsty again. You're going to have to keep coming back again and again" — meaning that the source and wellspring of her tradition aren't enough to satisfy her. What he is offering to give her is another kind of water altogether. If she drinks the water that he will offer to her, she will never again thirst for sustenance, source, meaning, depth, wisdom, and life. And he continues, saying that the living water that he will give her will "become in [her] a spring of water welling up to eternal life." If she drinks of his living water, she herself will become a fountain of living water in the midst of the desert, leaping up for all to drink from, even in the worst drought and heat of the day. It is too much. She wants the water he is offering to her. And her words are, "Sir, give me this water . . ." But she has no idea of the meaning and depth of his words, or of the gift he is offering her. She refers back to the water in the well to finish her plea — "so that I may not be thirsty or have to keep coming here to draw water." They are like two rivers crisscrossing each other but not really connecting at any depth.

This whole story is a process, a ritualized accounting of preparation for baptism and the sacraments of initiation for John's community. This woman of Samaria goes through the struggle for wisdom and the asking for baptism, the shift from her old traditions and heritage into the deeper sources of Scripture and finally into the presence and the person of Jesus, who is the Word of God made flesh, dwelling among us in the Scripture/the Gospels, in the waters of baptism and the oil of confirmation, in the bread and wine of the Eucharist, in the community of the Beloved Disciple — in the Body of Christ and in the waters of all the world's resources and presence. She has asked for baptism, but like all of us asking for baptism — living waters — she has no concept of what she is really asking for — or of the gift that God seeks to give to us. She is looking only for what she thinks will make her life easier: she won't have to keep coming to draw water daily — she'll have it herself, to herself.

But she has stepped into the waters, and the journey has begun. The waters of the Word of God in the Gospels, in Jesus dwelling among us in the mysterious presences of the Incarnation and the Resurrection and the gift of the Spirit in the world and in all who believe, even those who believe by their thirst for the Holy — these are now her way of being in the world. Her tradition will develop into the broader rivers of the heritage her people left behind when they chose to worship other gods along with the One God and betrayed the covenant with the nations who conquered them, including the Romans that they now incorporate into their lives, shunting aside the values and practices of their ancestral traditions handed on from Jacob and Joseph.

Her drinking of the living waters of Jesus begins with turning aside from the other idols, polluted rituals, and worship of others rather than only serving and obeying the God of life. In the continuation of the story, she will confess to the five husbands her nation of Samaria has lived with, accommodating the marriage of Yahweh and the people that were chosen to be witnesses of the worship of the Holy One with economics, politics, culture, and what afforded them an easier life. She will learn wisdom — what constitutes true worship of God, the care of the poor, and the coming of the realm of abiding justice that seeds long-lasting peace from the One she begins to see as a prophet. And she will leave her water jar at the well, having been baptized, and having drunk deep of Jesus' living water — the Word — and she will go back into her village to tell the story of who she has met. But her telling will reveal all that she did not catch, the water she drank without awareness or understanding, and how deep still is the well and the fountain that she has been drawn to by Jesus' words and presence.

In her words with the Word of God, she will ask him if he is the messiah — from her tradition — generally thought to be nationalistic, returning Jerusalem, the temple, and the nation to their former glory and driving the Romans out. And Jesus will refuse to use her words. His new language is that of the living waters of the Scriptures and his own body of living water. He tells her point-blank that "I AM is speaking to you." But she cannot hear. She went looking for a messiah, based on her past, and that's what she found and took back to her people and village. No single individual can know the wisdom of the Word that is spoken in Jesus or begin to know the wisdom of the Scriptures and the life within that is living water — the presence of God springing up within us to eternal life, here and now. The woman will tell her story, as fragmented as it is — a couple of drops in the oceans of water — and many will go out to listen to the Waters for themselves, and they will learn more than anything she could pick up and drink on her own — that he is more than messiah, more than anything they could imagine. He is, for beginners, the Savior of the whole world, and they will spend the rest of their lives drinking deep of the waters of the Word of God, in the Scriptures, in the presence of God in Jesus, in the waters of the world — the sacrament of the Spirit with each other . . . and someday they will begin to hear and drink from I AM!

Waters, words, wisdom, women, and the Word have a rich and long telling and experience. Later in John's Gospel, Jesus will cry out, "Let anyone who thirsts come to me and drink. Whoever believes in me, as scripture says: 'Rivers of living water will flow from within [them]'" (John 7:37b-39a). He says this in reference to the Spirit that those who came to believe in him would receive.

Not only is another world possible, she is on her way. On a quiet day, I can hear her breathing.

Arundhati Roy

Women and water have been bound together since the beginning of time. They are the water-drawers, those who water the fields and cook the food and clean. They live as close to water as they do to the earth, and they are the ones who rally when it is unjustly denied them and their families. Eduardo Galeano of Uruguay has written a number of books, collecting vignettes of history, insight, indignation, and hope that chronicle the history of such things as water, oil, gold, slavery, churches, sex, and land from the vantage point of those who didn't write the history books. Today he has hundreds of young people collecting the information for him — he arranges the bits and pieces to tell a story. Here are two that deal with water and women in the last five hundred years in South America:

Danger at the Tap

According to Revelation 21:6, God will create a new world and say, "I will give unto him that is athirst of the fountain of water of life freely."

Freely? Meaning the new world won't make room for the World Bank or the private companies that ply the noble trade in water?

So it seems. Meanwhile, in the old world where we all still live, sources of water are as coveted as oil reserves, and are becoming battlegrounds.

In Latin America, the first water war was the invasion of Mexico by Hernan Cortes. More recently, combat over the blue gold took place in Bolivia and Uruguay. In Bolivia, people took to the streets and won back their lost water. In Uruguay, the people voted in a plebiscite to keep their water from being lost.

Galeano adds this piece on the next page — supplementing the reality with a victory so that readers may take heart.

Danger in the Sky

In the year 2003, a tsunami of people washed away the government of Bolivia.

The poor were sick and tired. Everything had been privatized, even the rainwater. A "for sale" sign had been hung on Bolivia, and they were going to sell it, Bolivians and all.

The uprising shook El Alto, perched above the incredibly high city of La Paz, where the poorest of the poor work throughout their lives, day after day, chewing on their troubles. They are so high up they push the clouds when they walk, and every house has a door to heaven.

Heaven was where those who died in the rebellion went. It was a lot closer than earth. Now they are shaking up paradise.[3]

El Alto is the area above La Paz where the indigenous live by their ancient traditions, and it was these women who had had enough when they learned that the Bechtel Company had bought all the water in the city and now was selling it. Within weeks they were paying more for their privatized water supplies (primarily cached rainwater) than they were for rent and food and transportation. They rallied with flags, pots and pans, and songs, and went through the winding streets of town. They did plays in the plaza, making fun of the idiocy of what was happening, and within weeks they shut down the entire city and reclaimed their water. Then, and still today, Bechtel, a company that is connected with Cheney and others in the United States (it is also a major player in the dam projects of India), is suing the city of El Alto for 25 million in lost revenue. And the women of El Alto (at an elevation of more than 14,000 feet in the Andes) know the price of water — not to be sold, priceless — living water.

And there have been long rivers of women who have been intimately connected to waters of the earth, waters of wisdom and words. And there are women today standing deep in the river of that tradition. The woman whose words begin this chapter is one of them. She is Arundhati Roy. Her first book, *The God of Small Things,* won the Booker Prize. The story takes place in a small village in Kerala, India, and it is about caste, about children and about water too.[4] Roy has been an architect and a writer, but for the last several years she has gathered all her resources and knowledge and become the spokesperson for people in the central and western states of Madhya Pradesh, Maharashtra, and Gujarat, who are resisting the building and deployment of a series of dams that threaten the land, the villages and towns, the homes, and the very lives and way of life of tens of millions of Indians. Roy speaks often on behalf of the organization Narmada Bachao Andolan (NBA) that exists to protest the dam project. She stands with them, speaking out and getting arrested; she even gave her Booker Prize money ($30,000) to help them. Now, instead of writing novels, she writes to inform people worldwide about the issue of water and how economic, political, and national choices impact not only the future but the immediate present of hundreds of millions of people on earth. Her devastatingly truthful, pointed books, short and clear, have rallied masses of people but not endeared her to those in government and the upper castes.

In an interview with David Barsamian in *Lapis* magazine, she speaks about her writing:

> I don't see a great difference between *The God of Small Things* and my works of nonfiction. As I keep saying, fiction is truth. I think fiction is the truest thing there ever was. My whole effort now is to

remove that distinction. The writer is the midwife of understanding. It's very important for me to tell politics like a story, to make it real. That's what I want to do. *The God of Small Things* is a book where you connect the very smallest things to the very biggest: whether it's the dent that a baby spider makes on the surface of water or the quality of moonlight on a river or how history and politics intrude into your life, your house, your bedroom.[5]

Even the titles of Roy's recent books are provocative but clear on what the issues are and what's at stake in her own country and in most of the underdeveloped but drained-dry countries of the earth. The titles are words about life and its interconnectedness, beginning with her novel *The God of Small Things,* followed by *The Cost of Living.* They describe succinctly the huge gap between people and governments and institutions, crying out about the disregard for people, men and women and children, ordinary families. Next comes *An Ordinary Person's Guide to Empire,* where Roy moves past the borders of her own country — India — into the globalization of basic issues: water, dams, poverty, politics, caste and class, disease, the bases for war and the media's hand in it all. The book *The Checkbook and the Cruise Missile* is a collection of her interviews with David Barsamian, in which she looks at huge issues not just simply but truthfully as they impact each other and often become at odds with one another. The titles given to the interviews are illuminating: "Knowledge and Power," "Terror and the Maddened King," "Privatization and Polarization," and "Globalization of Dissent." These are all issues of the common good, common ground for all peoples, and Roy discusses both how to resist what is the reality for many in the world and how to seed the future with hope. Her latest book, *Power Politics,* deals with "the algebra of infinite justice," war and peace, and the bedrock and living waters of compassion, truthfulness, community dissent, and power that is nonviolent.[6]

Roy is aware of the responsibility she carries and the words she uses, in writing and in speaking. In *Power Politics,* she acknowledges that "there is an intricate web of morality, rigor, and responsibility that art, that writing itself, imposes on a writer." She continues,

. . . in the midst of putative peace, you could, like me, be unfortu-
nate enough to stumble on a silent war. The trouble is that once
you see it, you can't unsee it. And once you've seen it, keeping
quiet, saying nothing, becomes as political an act as speaking out.
There's no innocence. Either way, you're accountable.[7]

She speaks of globalization from the place where the majority of
people experience it — the bottom. She says, "Time to ask, in ordinary
language, the public question and to demand, in ordinary language,
the public answer."[8] She is clear about what globalization is —
whether the issue is water and dams, electricity and power, economics,
corporations, food, democracy, disease, terrorism, war, nationalism —
it "is one single idea, which is ultimately . . . Life is Profit."[9] She ends
her opening chapter with these stirring words:

Cynics say that real life is a choice between the failed revolution
and the shabby deal. I don't know . . . maybe they're right. But
even they should know that there's no limit to just how shabby
that shabby deal can be. What we need to search for and find,
what we need to hone and perfect into a magnificent, shining
thing, is a new land of politics. Not the politics of governance, but
the politics of resistance. The politics of opposition, the politics of
forcing accountability. The politics of slowing things down. The
politics of joining hands across the world and preventing certain
destruction. In the present circumstances, I'd say that the only
thing worth globalizing is dissent. It's India's best export.[10]

Roy not only is a member of the Narmada Bachao Andolan; she
speaks about them, organizing and inviting others to join. She speaks
of the NBA as being a cross-section of the Indian populace, made up of
Adivasis (indigenous people), upper-caste farmers, the Dalits (once
called the Untouchables), and the middle class. As she explains,

It's a forging of links between the urban and the rural, between the
farmers and the fishermen and the writers and the painters. That's
what gives it its phenomenal strength, and it's what a lot of people

criticize it for in India, saying, "These middle-class protestors!" That makes me furious. In many ways, people try to delegitimize the involvement of the middle class, saying, "How can you speak on behalf of these people?" No one is speaking on behalf of anyone. The point is that the NBA is a fantastic example of people linking hands across caste and class. It is the biggest, most magnificent resistance movement since the independence struggle.[11]

They say that Roy is the woman who first came up with the line "What we need is a globalization of compassion!" She began by observing the natural world, and the stream of living so intently drew her into larger and larger currents, until now she sees and speaks in communion with all those who struggle to live more humanly, to live beyond mere survival, to live with hope. Following is my favorite quote from her. I heard it on NPR a number of years ago. When I teach workshops on water, women, and wisdom, I often conclude with this quote, which is about what is important in life:

To love. To be loved. To never forget your own insignificance. To never get used to the unspeakable violence and vulgar disparity of life around you. To seek joy in the saddest places. To pursue beauty to its lair. To never simplify what is complicated or complicate what is simple. To respect strength, never power. Above all, to watch. To try and understand. To never look away. And never, never to forget.

As this book goes to press, Roy's new book, *Field Notes on Democracy: Listening to Grasshoppers,* has recently been published. It looks at issues like water, the loss of land, habitats, people's livelihoods, and property, massive poverty, escalating brutality, and the loss of human rights — all are grim realities in India. But Roy ends the book by talking about fighting — about resisting with everyone. As she said in an interview, "All of us are joined together by the determination that even if we lose, we're going to fight, you know? And we're not going to just let this happen without doing everything we can to stop it. And that gives me a tremendous amount of hope."[12]

Sources Used in This Chapter

Maggie Black. *The No-Nonsense Guide to Water.* Oxford, U.K.: New Internationalist Publications, 2004.

Greenpeace. *Planet Ocean: Thirty Postcards That Will Take You on a Worldwide Ocean Voyage.* Oxford, U.K.: New Internationalist Publications, 2007.

Arundhati Roy. *An Ordinary Person's Guide to Empire.* Cambridge, Mass.: South End Press, 2004.

Arundhati Roy. *The Checkbook and the Cruise Missile: Conversations with Arundhati Roy,* Interviews by David Barsamian. Cambridge, Mass.: South End Press, 2004.

Arundhati Roy. *The Cost of Living.* New York: The Modern Library, 1999.

Arundhati Roy. *Field Notes on Democracy: Listening to Grasshoppers.* London: Haymarket Books, 2009.

Arundhati Roy. *The God of Small Things.* New York: Harper Perennial, 1998.

Arundhati Roy. *Power Politics,* 2d ed. Cambridge, Mass.: South End Press, 2001.

Chapter 3

Trees, Genealogies, and Friends

The old pine tree teaches wisdom, and the cry of the wild bird expresses truth.

Zen koan

True friends are like seashells . . . they murmur endlessly.

Swahili proverb

Trees are called "the tall standing ones" among the native peoples of the Americas. They have their own language and connect many different groups: the birds, the weather, the day and night skies, the earth through their roots, and the many animals that come under their branches. If a person knows the language of the trees, he or she receives the knowledge that all these groups bring to the listening bark of the trees, and is honored for knowing the interconnectedness of many parts of the world. It is taught that each of us has a "spirit tree," an actual tree that dwells in our environs (within walking distance) that is the visible symbol of our inner soul at any one time. Once we know our spirit trees, we can visit, observe, reflect on, and learn from them how to deal with our daily lives and transform them into what is more whole for everyone around us.

This sense of trees' power, their rootedness and centrality to an environment, is universal. In many European countries, the tree that stands alone in the middle of a field or an ancient standing tree roots the water and nutrients, even the spirits of everything growing around it. The health of that tree reflects the health of everything bound to it. In ancient times, the woods were the places of worship, of gathering, and of the rituals that honored and noted the seasons of the crops and the seasons of human life: seedtime, rain, and harvest; engagements, marriages, births, and deaths. And in Africa, many tribes gather beneath the spreading canopy of the trees not just for shade and shelter; they gather under the trees' umbrella to do business, honor contracts, and make peace. There is an African proverb that reminds them of the relationship of their own lives to the earth: "In the forest, when the branches quarrel, the roots embrace."

In all of Central and South America and in many Asian countries, trees are living beings, akin to humans, to be honored, respected, tended, and cut down only when necessary — and even then, the ritual of the cutting and felling of the tree follows ancient customs. These are the words of Artemildo Ribeiro da Silva, a Brazilian forest doctor (b. 1965): "Most people see only trees and leaves and plants and animals, but I see remedies and cures for all the diseases of the world — almost all. The forest has the answers."

For the ancient Israelites and for Christians, trees stand at the beginning and the end of sacred scriptures and serve as markers, great symbols throughout the Testaments. The first time Abraham "sees" YHWH, the Torah portion is called "Vayeira," from its first word, which is usually translated "appeared." The second word is YHWH, usually translated "LORD," but with no vowels written or uttered, it can be pronounced only like one is consciously breathing. In one of his online teachings, Rabbi Arthur Waskow calls this second word "Breath of Life" or "Wind/ Breath/Spirit of the world."[1] This portion of Genesis 18:1–22:24 binds together trees — the oaks of Mamre — Abraham's being able to "see" the Lord, and the announcement to Abraham and Sarah that they would have a child. Waskow's commentary and exegesis are powerful:

> The first sentence says "YHWH brought-about-being-*seen* to [Abraham] in [*b'*] the oaks of Mamre."

Then the story continues: ". . . and he lifted up his eyes and *saw [va'yar]* and here! — three people were standing upon him, and he *saw [va'yar]* and ran . . . [to bring-them-near and then to feed them]."

First, the oak trees themselves and then the three visitors were the visible, see-able presence of God. How can the Divine Breathing-Spirit of the world become visible in trees? Think about the rustling leaves, quivering as the wind rushes from them, in them, into them. Quivering as the trees breathe out what we breathe in (oxygen), and then breathe in what we breathe out (carbon dioxide). This is the rhythm of life upon our planet. As we open our eyes to this rush of breath, we see God. It was not till Abraham saw God breathing in these oak trees that Abraham was able to see God breathing in human beings.

And then the story in Genesis continues with Abraham and Sarah feeding the three strangers (feeding God!) and sharing with others the abundance of life that they have been given. And when the guests have eaten, they give the good news to Abraham (Sarah is listening at the tent's open flap) that when they come again, Abraham and Sarah will have a child. Rabbi Waskow says,

> Not till he [Abraham] saw God in this body of earth-human interchange could his and Sarah's bodies intertwine to seed new life. (Till then, Sarah had been an *akarah* — a "root" without a sprouting. Perhaps it was not she who was barren; perhaps her rootedness needed some new quickening in Abraham, this vision more connected to the earth, to make her root more fruitful.)

So if this story honors the first expression of eco-Judaism (and maybe eco-Christianity and eco-Islam, all born of Abraham's vision), we should honor this story by opening our eyes to it.

Look closely at a tree, at grass. Sniff at its leaves, breathing life into it and out of it. Pray not to the tree but to the whispering, rustling Breath that enters it and leaves it. Promise to sustain it. ACT to sustain it.[2]

This vital connection between trees of the earth and humans being seeded and born from generation to generation is not as foreign as we might think. After all, we all trace our families' roots and ancestry back in time, place, names, and bondings and call them family trees — genealogies. Our existence upon the earth and our continuous existence are perhaps more intimately bound to the trees of the world than we are aware of, or appreciate. Our bodies and our souls stand and fall with the bodies and souls of our planet's trees. There is an old story from the Jewish traditions of Eastern Europe in the late nineteenth century that is called "The Souls of Trees." It is one of the stories of Reb Nachman of Bratslav, one of the leaders of the Hasidic movement which used stories, music and dancing, and discipline and discipleship to know the mysteries of the Holy ever more deeply. This is how I tell it.

Once upon a time, Reb Nachman gave orders to his coachman and his disciples to get ready — they were going on a trip. His usual words were all he told them: "Someone is in great need of our presence and help." And they were off. But it was a strange trip because the Reb told his coachman to let the horses go where they wanted to go — and not to lead them!

The trip took all day, but the horses were sure-footed and seemed to know exactly where to go. Night came on, and the disciples were hungry and wondering where they would spend the night. Reb Nachman only said what he always did: "The Holy One will provide — remember that." Just then they rounded a corner and found themselves at an inn owned by a Jewish couple. They were welcomed graciously and treated with respect and honor. They prayed together. They ate together. They studied Torah together. They drank together. They prayed again together. It was late when the innkeeper finally led them all to their rooms. The Reb was the last to go, and the innkeeper drew him aside and asked for counsel. The Reb knew right away what the man would speak about, for he had not seen any children in the inn. And so it was, as the man told his story. He and his wife had been married for ten years, and they loved one another dearly, but God had not blessed them with any children. Was there anything that they could do? Was there anything that he, the rabbi, could do for them? Reb

Nachman was tired and asked to sleep on it and to pray on it; they would talk again in the morning light.

Reb Nachman was tired and fell asleep instantly, but in the middle of the night he awoke crying and weeping. Everyone ran to see what was wrong, and they found the rabbi sitting up in bed with a book in his hand, pointing to a passage and reading it softly over and over again. He looked up and said, "Go back to bed. I'm fine. Bless the Holy One." They all went back to bed, but the innkeeper and his wife didn't sleep a wink. In the morning everyone rose as usual and said their prayers. Then Reb Nachman stood to speak with the innkeeper and his wife alone. There was silence — tense and full. And the Reb asked them solemnly, "Tell me, did you build the walls of this inn with saplings that were cut down before their time?"

Husband and wife looked at each other and back to the Rabbi: "Yes, but how did you know?"

The Reb sighed and told them. "All night I dreamed that I was enclosed by the bodies of the dead crying out with no other recourse. When I awoke crying, I picked up a book and read this line: 'Cutting down a tree before its time is the same as killing a soul.' I realized then that all night I was surrounded by the souls of the trees crying. And I realized why you and your wife have had no children." The couple looked distressed but did not understand.

Reb Nachman continued, "There is an angel, Lailah, the angel of conception, who waits, and at the appropriate time she brings the soul of the yet-to-be-born child to its parents. But every time Lailah approaches your home, she is driven back by the pain and cries of the souls of the trees that were cut down too soon. And so she leaves, carrying her blessing still with her." The husband and wife were stunned.

But Reb Nachman smiled. "There is a remedy! You must plant trees, twice as many trees as you cut down for the inn. Honor the trees and walk in the grove and do not cut them down. Do this for the next three years, and Lailah will be able to come to you with the Holy One's blessing of a child."

The Reb and his disciples left that day, watching the couple plant trees. For three years the couple obeyed and planted trees, in rows, at random, in pockets along the road, in the fields. And in three years' time, Lailah came again with the blessing. This time it was as though the angel was soothed by a lullaby of young trees murmuring and whispering that was stronger than the cries and whimpering of the souls of the trees severed before their time. It is said that every year after that, Lailah came, to make up for the lost years and the lost trees — and that all the children stood straight and grew tall and strong, lithe and graceful like the trees. And that the first thing they all learned was to plant trees, to protect the trees and visit them in awe, listening to the singing, breathing, and praying of the trees.

This story leaves nothing unsaid. The question is, Do we honor the trees of the earth? If we are honest, most of the time most of us don't — trees are commodities, useful for everything from houses and furniture to firewood and railroad ties. Sadly, we even cut down giant redwoods and sequoias to make disposable chopsticks! At best, we make lists of the ten best trees to have in our houses to help with air quality. Or on a larger scale we dedicate areas of land and trees for national parks, though we haven't designated any new parks in ages. What are we leaving as a legacy, as companions, as shade and shelter, beauty and soul to our children and the generations after us?

There is a book in the Old Testament named after a woman, Ruth, that looks at trees and souls, genealogy and children. The book should be called "Ruth and Naomi" because more to the point, it is a book about friendship and the making of new roots, trees, descendants, and children. It is the story of two widows, two women, two friends, from two countries, one born to Judaism and the other a convert. We forget that their story and their words are the source and root of wedding vows and marriage rituals — words spoken not between a man and a woman but between two women. And these women are poor, strangers, refugees returning home, immigrants, migrants, scavengers, gleaning the fields of others, grieving the loss of their husbands and the loss of a future because they are childless. Perhaps the book is named specifically after Ruth because of her tender regard for and support of her mother-in-law, or because she saves a bloodline in Israel, or because she accepts the Torah, the Word of God, and her life is seeded in the promise given to the people of Israel as her womb will be seeded with her own child.

This book of Ruth is read — all night — on the second night of the feast of Shavuot, the feast day that remembers and honors the giving of the Torah to the people on Mount Sinai. This evokes the history of the people who received the Torah, the Word of God, and yet wandered in the desert, as a lost generation, because they were unwilling to take hold of the covenant and live it — and so never entered the land promised to them. Yearly the people are reminded now not to follow them, but to be like Ruth, committing themselves to the study of and obedience to the Torah and its laws, its memory, its traditions, and its hope in the future.

The story begins with Orpah and Ruth, both Moabites, and Naomi starting back to Naomi's land of Bethlehem in Judah — a place they had originally fled because of famine. Naomi laments her losses, the loss of her two sons, Orpah and Ruth's husbands, and the grandchildren they would have given to her. After they have begun their journey, she tells both Orpah and Ruth to go back to their people. Orpah decides to return, but Ruth decides to stay with her mother-in-law. The three women weep and kiss as they part. We are told that "Ruth clung to her" (Naomi).

Ruth's words in response to Naomi's repeated urging that she leave with Orpah are poignant, powerful, and intimately moving, the essence of lovingkindness and devotion. Ruth shows *hesed* (the Hebrew word for fidelity), loving compassion, and tenderness that goes far beyond any obedience to the law, thus mirroring one of the strongest characteristics of Yahweh. It is worth noting that God isn't really mentioned, but the presence of the Holy One is like the shade and the shadow of a tree, extending protection over all and standing there with them, in every moment and place, in each decision and experience of just being human.

God is with them as Ruth offers Naomi commitments and pronouncements of love. She speaks words beyond comfort:

"Do not urge me to leave you, to turn back and not follow you. For wherever you go, I will go; wherever you lodge, I will lodge; your people shall be my people, and your God my God. Where you die, I will die, and there I will be buried. Thus and more may the LORD do to me if anything but death parts me from you." When [Naomi] saw how determined she was to go with her, she ceased to argue with her; and the two went on until they reached Bethlehem. (Ruth 1:16-19)

They have chosen Bethlehem because they are desperate for food, and Naomi has distant cousins in the land who must obey the laws of letting those in need glean the fields before a second cutting. And perhaps her cousin Boaz will also obey the Levirate law of marriage: the requirement that a kinsman marry the widow who is fatherless to raise up children to her husband's memory, name, and legacy.

Naomi and Ruth arrive in Bethlehem ("the House of Bread") at the beginning of the barley harvest. And when Naomi (her name means "pleasant") returns, they welcome her, but she cries out, "Do not call me Naomi. Call me Mara, for Shaddai has made my lot very bitter. I went away full, and the LORD has brought me back empty."

And immediately we are told of Boaz (his name means "in him is strength"), Naomi's kinsman, who is a man of substance with a large field. And mother and daughter-in-law (now just called "daughter," familiarly and tenderly — her name means "friend or companion") begin gleaning and gathering behind the reapers. It is Ruth who stays at it morning to night, and Boaz comes to her, telling her to stay and reap in his field, drink of his water, and rest when she needs to. He tells her that he has heard of her kindness to his kinswoman, Naomi. And he calls down Yahweh's blessings upon her: "May the LORD reward your deeds. May you have a full recompense from the LORD, the God of Israel, under whose wings you have sought refuge" (Ruth 2:12). And we learn after the day's work and the meal she shared with the workers that Ruth has no idea who Boaz is. And she continues to work in the fields with his maidservants and to stay at home with her mother-in-law.

Later, Ruth obeys Naomi's instructions on how to approach Boaz when the harvest is complete. It is worth mentioning that what she does in preparation for the meeting, in hopes of marriage, reflects the stages of ritual conversion to Judaism and dedication to the Torah. Her passionate response to Naomi is considered by the rabbis to be her declaration of the beginning of the formal process of conversion, meaning "not even death will part us." The commentary in the Jewish Study Bible tells us this:

> According to Rashi, following [y. Pe'ah 8.7], Ruth's preparations [are] related directly to her conversion. In washing herself, Ruth purified herself from her earlier idolatry; in anointing herself, she took upon herself the commandments; in dressing, she put on Sabbath garments, that is, full observance of the Sabbath. (p. 1583)

Boaz accepts Ruth's invitation (and her proposal of marriage, which is an action that goes beyond any understanding of law) and in public calls for witnesses to his marriage. In doing so, he not only takes Ruth as his wife but also acquires all that belonged to Chilion and Mahlon (Naomi's sons). The reason he gives for doing this is clear: "so as to perpetuate the name of the deceased upon his estate, that the name of the deceased may not disappear from among his kinsmen and from the gate of his home town. You are witnesses today" (Ruth 4:10). Children, land, and marriage are all braided into one piece. What follows is the witnesses' blessing upon Ruth:

> All the people at the gate and the elders answered, "May the LORD make the woman who is coming into your house like Rachel and Leah, both of whom built up the House of Israel! Prosper in Ephrathah and perpetuate your name in Bethlehem! And may your house be like the house of Perez, whom Tamar bore to Judah — through the offspring which the LORD will give you by this young woman." (Ruth 4:11-12)

The book moves quickly to a denouement. A generation has been saved, and a line of the tree of life in Israel has been redeemed. In her marriage to Boaz, Ruth conceives a son, Obed. And the women relate to Naomi and the child, honoring the friendship and the tie between these two women, and they bless Yahweh with these words:

> Blessed be the LORD, who has not withheld a redeemer from you today! May his name be perpetuated in Israel! He will renew your

45

life and sustain your old age; for he is born of your daughter-in-law, who loves you and is better to you than seven sons!

This is high praise for Ruth, and it honors the bond of the two women. The story ends with these words: "They [the women] named him Obed; he was the father of Jesse, father of David." And then follows the genealogy in the line of Perez (Boaz's ancestors and progeny; Ruth 4:17-22). Ruth's stock, a foreigner who images the attributes of the Holy, has been grafted onto the tree of life in Israel, and from her will come forth the future of the people. The notes in the Jewish Study Bible put it clearly, with all of its consequences:

> The genealogy draws a direct line between Perez (son of Tamar) through Obed (son of Ruth) to David. In this way the theme of family continuity and divine favor through Ruth is extended to embrace national continuity and divine favor through David. The genealogy also helps to frame the book, which opens with Bethlehem, the home of David, and concludes with the genealogy of David. (p. 1586)

And so the tree's roots go deep and long. And generations and hundreds of years will pass, and another genealogy will be written that traces a direct line from Abraham to Perez (whose mother is Tamar) to Salmon, the father of Boaz (whose mother is Rahab), who marries Ruth (the mother of Obed and the great, great, great . . . grandmother of David, the king). And the genealogy will continue through Solomon (whose mother is not mentioned by name; she was the wife of Uriah, who was killed so that she could marry David), through the remnants of the Babylon exile, and down through Jacob, the father of Joseph, the husband of Mary, the mother of Jesus, the Messiah. The tree's roots reach backward to the beginning of faith in Judaism and stretch forward to the beginning of faith in Christianity and continue on through the prophet Jesus in Islam.

But what would happen if Ruth and Naomi came today to the United States, or other countries, or western or eastern Europe? This is a story of reverse immigration and migration; famine and poverty;

sickness, deaths in families, and the making of widows; bonding beyond blood and marriage ties to make new kinship bonds; the desire for children, for a name, for life with dignity, for hope for the future. It is a story of hope for compassion and lovingkindness *(hesed)* in the face of living on the road, crossing borders, scavenging for leftovers (not much different from rooting through garbage bins), and taking care of each other when you find you have fallen through the cracks of the system, through the way it is supposed to work and provide for the common good of all.

Again the Jewish rabbi Arthur Waskow asks this question, and then answers it with more questions, summoning us to reflect and do theology, look at our economics and politics, demanding that we be honest in our responses and our responsibilities:

> But — if Ruth came to America today, what would happen? Would she be admitted at the border? Or would vigilantes chase her through the desert, fire rifles at her, leave her dying of thirst?
>
> Would she have to show a "green card" before she could get a job gleaning at any farm, restaurant, or hospital — and if so, how could she get such permission?
>
> Would she be sent to a detention center for years while her application for asylum was "considered"?
>
> Would she be sent to "workfare" with no protections for her dignity, her freedom, or her health?
>
> Would she face contempt because she and Naomi, traveling without a man, might be a lesbian couple?
>
> When she boldly "uncovers the feet" of Boaz . . . has she violated the "family values" that some religious folk now proclaim?
>
> . . . Because Ruth and Boaz, the outcast and the solid citizen, got together, they became the ancestors of King David. And therefore of [the] Messiah, the transformation that brings peace and justice to the world.
>
> And it's not just Ruth and Boaz. The Book of Ruth goes out of its way to establish that Boaz's ancestry goes back to Judah and Tamar (Gen. 38) . . . [Because Judah refuses to marry Tamar, she seduces him, pretending to be a prostitute so that she can have children —

this is Boaz's heritage too.] From their transgressive sexual connection came forth not only King David but, according to tradition, David's heir — the Messiah.

And Ruth came from a similar lineage. She was a Moabite, a descendant of Moab. And who was he? The child of Lot, who had been seduced by one of his daughters after she concluded that the volcanic destruction of Sodom and Gomorrah meant that all men in the world had died and she could find no other husband by whom to raise a child (Gen. 19:30-38).

So we have this triad of women, outsiders, seemingly transgressors, who affirmed a higher good — their own right to a decent place in society, to children — against the conventional social "decency."[3]

So, in light of our family trees and our religious genealogies, what are our duties and responsibilities to our relatives and our fellow human beings today as Jews, as Christians, as human beings? The women and children of our family trees, the immigrants and migrants, the refugees, the homeless, the hungry, those who break our cultural and religious laws because of their needs and their humanness, those who are widows and orphans — what do we owe them? Is it time that we look at the limbs and branches we are severing and chopping off? Is it time to return to our roots as family? And in doing so, look around at our trees, our ancient standing ancestors, and what we are doing to them. Are we cutting ourselves off from the future as we massively destroy those standing in our presence today?

> *The earth was naked.*
> *For me the mission was to try to cover it with green.*
>
> Wangari Maathai

Perhaps the woman most associated with trees in this decade is Wangari Maathai of Kenya, who has received the Nobel Peace Prize for her environmentalism, her planting of trees, and her vision and organizing of women to make sure there is a future for the coming generations. Maathai was born in the village of Ihithe, in the forested lands of Nyeri, Kenya, in 1940. She remembers a childhood in the fields and the forests, with birds and maize, sweet potatoes and fertile soils. She was awarded scholarships and went to school in the United States, where she got her BA and her MA in biological sciences. And then she came home to East Africa and was the first woman to be awarded a PhD from the University of Nairobi. After completing her doctorate, she started teaching — not just courses in the university but lessons on how to empower people, especially women, to protect the environment and their own health and that of their families against clear-cutting, commercial logging, and plantations of trees that were not native but raised as cash crops. In 1976 and 1977, she was named chair of the Department of Veterinary Anatomy at the University of Nairobi and then associate professor of that department. It was the first time that either position was given to a woman.

Over the next decade, from 1976 to 1987, she was a member of the National Council of the Women of Kenya. She came to realize that the women are being cut off from their basic food crops, from the land, and that poverty is bound to the environment as well as to social and economic realities. In an interview with Amitabh Pal in *The Progressive* magazine, she spoke of the overlapping realities that impact people, politics, land, food, and the future:

> Poverty is both a cause and a symptom of environmental degradation. You can't say you'll deal with just one. It's a trap. When you're in poverty, you're trapped because the poorer you become, the more you degrade the environment, and the more you degrade the environment, the poorer you become. So it's a matter of breaking the cycle.
>
> We cannot solve all the problems we face: we don't have water, we don't have energy, we don't have food, we don't have incomes, we're not able to send our children to school. But we can do *some-thing* — something that is cheap, that is within our power, our capacity, our resources. And planting a tree was the best idea I had. For me, it became a wonderful way of breaking the cycle.[4]

In 1977 this idea was seeded and began to grow into the Green Belt Movement, a grassroots organization dedicated to working with

49

women's groups to plant trees that will both improve their lives and stop the destruction of their environments. By 1986 the Green Belt Movement expanded and branched out into the Pan-African Green Belt Network and was planted in Tanzania, Ethiopia, Zimbabwe, Uganda, and Lesotho, and it continues to spread through Africa. (The statistics of 2005 state that the women have planted more than thirty million trees on their lands, around schools, churches, and homes.) And Maathai moved more publicly into connecting the issues of environmental destruction, poverty, national debts, globalization, development, economic scarcity, and the buying of African lands for "re-allocations" with illegal seizures and appropriations, stealing the land from the people for business corporations.

And she learned hard and fast that speaking the truth, standing with the trees as well as the women of the world, was dangerous. She was jailed, beaten, tortured, prosecuted, harassed, threatened, and attacked. But the long years of working with communities for democracy as well as encouraging women to plant trees and reforest their land so that they could plant food crops and retain water began to see results. In 2002 there were free elections in Kenya for the first time in a generation, and she was elected to parliament with an astounding 98 percent of the vote. And then she was appointed deputy minister for the environment.

In 2004, Maathai was awarded the Nobel Prize. The story is told that on the day she learned she had won the prize, she was on her way to Nyeri, her parliamentary district in central Kenya, and after weeping a bit, she knelt down on the ground, her hands in the red dirt, and planted a tree in gratitude — a Nandi flame tree in the shadow of Mount Kenya.

In a 2009 interview with Maathai on "Speaking of Faith," Krista Tippett described Maathai's spirit and soul — what lies underground and sources her work, her life, and her visions:

> My curiosity, of course, always drives towards the spiritual and ethical questions and convictions that drive human action. In the course of this conversation, Wangari Maathai describes the faith behind her ecological passion — a lively fusion of Christianity, real-

50

world encounters with good and evil, and the ancestral Kikuyu traditions of Kenya's central highlands. She grew up there, schooled by Catholic missionaries, and she remains a practicing Catholic to this day. But life has taught her to value anew the Kikuyu culture of her family's ancestry. The Kikuyu traditionally worshiped under trees and honored Mount Kenya — Africa's second-highest mountain — as the place where God resides. That mountain, as Wangari Maathai only later understood scientifically, is the source of most of Kenya's rivers. And the fig trees considered most sacred by the Kikuyu — those it was impermissible to cut down — had the deepest roots, bringing water from deep below the earth to the surface. Climate change has created a volatile ecology across the Horn of Africa, and this is compounded by the fact that those trees have been cut away systematically for decades, along with millions of others, by colonial Christians as well as African industrialists.

We in the West are in the process of relearning something that Wangari Maathai, from the vantage point of Africa, has known all along: ecology is a matter of life and death, peace and war. In awarding her the Nobel Peace Prize, the Norwegian Nobel committee noted that "when we analyze local conflicts, we tend to focus on their ethnic and religious aspects. But it is often the underlying ecological circumstances that bring the more readily visible factors to the flashpoint." In places as far-flung as the Sudan, the Philippines, Mexico, Haiti, and the Himalayas, deforestation, encroaching desert, and soil erosion are among the present root causes of civil unrest and war. Wangari Maathai has cited a history of inequitable distribution of natural resources, especially land, as a key trigger in last year's Kenyan post-election violence.[5]

It is now another six years since Maathai received the Nobel Peace Prize, and she travels the world, seeking to broaden the concept of peace as intimately bound to poverty, to trees, to ecology, to people's basic survival needs. In a piece she wrote for the thirty-fifth anniversary and celebration of Earth Day, she says, "Nature is not an amenity to be drawn upon. It is a fundamental component of our ability to survive — and a central pillar in expanding the possibilities for peace."

And she introduces her comments with a response to what she thought the Nobel Committee was trying to say to the world with her prize: "The message the committee sent was this: If we want a peaceful world, we have to manage our environment responsibly and sustainably. We also have to share natural resources equitably at local, national, and global levels."[6]

How? Again she has an answer. She speaks of a trip to Japan where she learned a new word and a new concept: *mottainai:*

> One meaning in Japanese is "what a waste." But it also captures in one term the "Three Rs" that environmentalists have been campaigning on for a number of years: reduce, reuse, and recycle.
>
> I am seeking to make *mottainai* a global campaign, adding one more "R" suggested by Klaus Topfer, the head of the UN Environment Program: "repair" resources where necessary.
>
> We can practice *mottainai* in rich countries where overconsumption is rampant, and we can do it in regions where environmental devastion is causing the poor to get poorer and the ecosystems on which they depend to be degraded, some beyond repair.
>
> In my case, *mottainai* means continuing to plant trees, particularly now that the long rains have come to Kenya.[7]

This is what Maathai exhorts as a way to practice and celebrate Earth Day every day. And she goes on to say that she will call on her government to use both sides of sheets of paper, thus halving the amount they use, and to stop use of plastic bags. Instead, she will call for the revitalization of traditional basket and cloth weaving, so that goods woven from sustainably harvested sisal plants can be sold to developed countries at a fair price. This would contribute to the earth's sustainability, to the livelihood of rural communities, to fair trade, and to an appreciation of ancestral wisdom. And Maathai extends a call — to all of us, nationally and locally, even in our religious gatherings — to start doing something now, this earth day. She ends with the story of a hummingbird — a story that is told in Japan, India, Pakistan, and many other countries. It is short and simple. This is the way she tells it, heard from someone in Japan:

When the forest where the hummingbird lived went up in flames, the other animals ran out to save themselves. But the humming-bird stayed, flying to and from a nearby river with drops of water in its beak to pour on the fire. From a distance, the other animals laughed and mocked it. "What do you think you're doing?" they shouted. "This fire is overwhelming. You can't do anything." Finally the hummingbird turned to them and said, "I'm doing what I can." So, this Earth Day, and every day, let us dedicate our-selves to making *mottainai* a reality, not just a slogan. We can all be like the hummingbird, doing whatever we can.

And for all of us it is time to plant trees native to our place. Perhaps we can begin with one for each of our ancestors, those who have gone before us in our particular faith and religious practice, and one for each of our children and grandchildren — down to the seventh gener-ation, as the Native Peoples say. And then we need to plant trees with those we are in conflict with as a sign of peace and the beginnings of the seed of a new future without violence, without poverty, and with-out outsiders — human beings lost to the future, either severed from or hanging by a leaf to the tree of life today.

I will end with a vision for the future, gleaned from the past (based on the Talmud Ta'anit 23a). It is a short story simply called "The Carob Tree."

Once upon a time, there was a pious man, Honi, who studied and prayed the psalms line by line. He dug into their meanings, seeking to plant their insights into his own life. But one line in one of the psalms disturbed him deeply: "When the LORD restored the fortunes of Zion — 'we saw it as in a dream' — our mouths were filled with laughter, our tongues, with songs of joy" (Ps. 126:1-2). Honi did a lot of think-ing about that line. The Exile lasted seventy years! Did it mean that the people, each of them, all of them, had held onto the dream for that long? For him and all those who prayed the psalm now (it is the psalm that's said as grace at all the Sabbath meals), did it mean that they were to live on their dreams for seventy years?

And then one day as he was walking from one village to another, he saw a family — father, mother, and four children — planting a tree. It looked like a carob tree. He walked over to them and asked, "How long does it take for this tree to bear fruit?"

And the mother answered, "Seventy years."

Honi was stunned and blurted out, "How can you be sure that you'll be here in seventy years to eat of its fruit?"

And she responded, "Sir, we found carob trees heavy with fruit in our families' groves and along the roads when we were children. We must make sure that our children and their children will know the fruit of the carob tree too, and we honor our ancestors' gifts to us in planting this tree."

This echoes a line from Maathai's acceptance speech for her Nobel Prize:

> We are called to assist the Earth to heal her wounds and in the process heal our own — indeed, to embrace the whole creation in all its diversity, beauty, and wonder.

Sources Used in This Chapter

Grace and Truth: A Journal of Catholic Reflection for Southern Africa 25, no. 1 (April 2008): "Ecology and the Environment" issue. See especially "Wangari Maathai and Other Ecological Prophets" by Rev. Dr. Andrew E. Warmback, pp. 13-23; and "Wangari Maathai — Nobel Lecture," pp. 23-29. See wency@sjti.ac.za or gracetruth@sjti.ac.za.

Wangari Maathai. *Unbowed: A Memoir.* New York: Alfred A. Knopf, 2006.

The People Who Hugged the Trees. Adapted by Deborah Lee Rose. West Cork, Ireland: Roberts Rinehart, Inc., 1990. This is a children's version of the story of the Chipko Movement and Amrita Devi of Rajasthan, India.

Jeanette Winter. *Wangari's Trees of Peace: A True Story from Africa.* New York: Harcourt, 2008.

Chapter 4

"Them" — Other Bridges to the Holy

If you have come here to help me, you are wasting your time . . .
but if you have come because your liberation is bound up with
mine, then let us work together.

Lilla Watson, aboriginal educator and activist

We live in a world of borders, boundaries, walls, and fear of differences: those who are "them" or "other" — other religions, other languages, other countries, other cultures, other races, other histories, and other perceptions. We often describe ourselves as "not this or that" rather than beginning with something that is human and shared by all human beings, no matter where they find themselves geographically, religiously, culturally, or socially. We look at many others askance, sideways, questioning, fearful, cynical, and even hostile, without ever really seeing them or coming to know them. There is a Buddhist koan (a teaching story), a parable that catches us in the truth — that startles and shocks us even — as other people often do. Men and women have struggled with this koan and the truthfulness and clear-seeing that it demands down through the ages. Now it is time for it to trip us up!

Once upon a time, Buddha was traveling to another country, and he sat down under a tree by a bridge to rest. He drank water and began to meditate and to doze a little in the shade of the tree, lulled by the sound of the running water. Buddha was getting old, and he was sitting cross-legged, comfortable and looking much like the fat Buddha statues, his stomach spreading over his legs. A samurai warrior on horseback came riding up and stopped to get water before crossing the bridge. He saw Buddha sitting there and roared out loud with laughter. Buddha opened his eyes and looked up at the man. He cocked his head at him, wondering what had caused the great laugh. The man looked at him again, laughing, and said, "You look like a huge pig!"

Buddha was silent for a moment, then looked up at the samurai and said solemnly, "And you look like God!"

The samurai was stunned and didn't know what to say. He pulled himself up to his full height and asked, "Really?"

"Yes," said Buddha, smiling at him.

"What in me, in my bearing, makes you say that I look like God?" the samurai asked.

"Oh," Buddha answered, "I spend most of my time in contemplation, looking for God. For years that is all I have tried to do, and now all I see is God!"

The samurai was quiet, trying to take that into his mind. But Buddha continued, "And you — what do you spend your time looking for? What do you see?"

And the story says that the samurai turned, mounted his horse, and left as quickly as he had come.

The story takes an unexpected turn — right out of nowhere. Most of us would consider ourselves religious people, or at least describe ourselves as seeking God, seeking to obey God's will, or seeking to live humanly and in accord with our faith's teachings and values — no matter what religion we would profess to believe and practice. And yet some of the strongest hostilities — even hatreds — and widest gaps in communication are among those of us who all avow that we believe in God and are fervent devotees of the faith communities that we belong to and worship God in together. How can this be? How can there be such a disconnect between seeking God, or seeing God, and not seeing other human beings clearly or even kindly, as human beings just like us, struggling to live with hope, with freedom, and in obedience to God? Sadly, this disconnect seems to be strongest among the three religions of the Book: Judaism, Christianity, and Islam. It is as though we are all porcupines, same species but different colors, and our usual posture toward everyone else is distance, suspicion, anger, and disdain. We don't even show a good deal of carefulness — an awareness of our own prickliness as well as theirs.

How do we look at one another — and what do we see when we approach one another? Why do we look upon our own so differently (more compassionately, giving them the benefit of the doubt, or accommodating their differences) than we do those of other faiths, other countries and races, other histories, other genders and social status? There is a disturbing story in the Gospels about Jesus being singled out by a foreigner, a woman, while he is traveling outside of Israel. The story is found halfway through the Gospel of Matthew (chapter 15:21-31), where we are told that "Jesus went from that place [Israel/Palestine] and withdrew [retreated] to the region of Tyre and Sidon. And a Canaanite woman [sometimes described as Syro-Phoenician] from that district" starts calling out to him and trailing along behind him. (The Canaanites were the original inhabitants of the land before the Israelites came out of the desert and claimed it as their own promised inheritance. They fought the Canaanites, conquering them and driving them out.) Jesus has left his own country; it appears that he is deliberately leaving and is seeking a refuge or a place of retreat. The word *withdrew* has the connotations of a military maneuver — withdrawing forces to reconnoiter and regroup.

Jesus has been preaching and teaching, going from village to village, from synagogue to synagogue, calling the people to be converted in their hearts, to repent and to come and follow him in obedience to the ancient words of the prophets and his bold proclamation of what that means for them in their lives. He has called them to no retaliation, no violence, to love of enemies, to care for the poor, to no judging of others, and to having hearts that are consonant with their actions. He ministers to great crowds — with hope, with healing, with food that he eats with them — sharing what he has given so freely to them with all others. He has taught them a depth and a spirit of obedience to the laws of Moses and called them to holiness, but he is roundly rejected by everyone — the chief priests, the scribes, the law-

57

yers, his own people, the people of his own hometown (Nazareth), his family; even his disciples are confused and keeping their distance from him, not understanding what he is saying but picking up on the rejection of so many around them. Being attached to Jesus as a disciple or just being in his presence is proving to be a hostile place to be found. The people who do listen, respond, and obey his admonitions to change are not the ones you would expect or hope for: a woman burdened with hemorrhaging for years, a demoniac from the Gadarenes (an area outside of Israel), a centurion of Rome, a grieving synagogue official on behalf of his dying daughter. But, generally speaking, whole towns, whole groups of people, and all the leaders — even his own relatives — are unrepentant, without faith, and angrily debate him and his words.

Jesus is battered and saddened by the reaction he is provoking in so many. What is happening? Why are they not listening and truly hearing and taking his words to heart? When this story begins, he has just come from a particularly virulent arguing session with the Pharisees, scribes, and elders.

> Then Jesus went from that place and withdrew to the region of Tyre and Sidon. And behold, a Canaanite woman from that district came and called out, "Have pity on me, Lord, Son of David! My daughter is tormented by a demon." But he did not say a word in answer to her. His disciples came and urged him, "Send her away, for she keeps calling out after us." He said in reply, "I was sent only to the lost sheep of the house of Israel." But the woman came and did him homage, saying, "Lord, help me." (Matt. 15:21-25)

It is important to get a sense of the scene that is so carefully set up before Jesus and the woman speak to each other. Jesus is outside Israel, with his disciples, and he is trying to stay away, or get away, from people, from the crowds who want his healing and help, but do not want to hear his words or shift their ways of living. He and his disciples are in another region, and the last thing they want is to be singled out, pointed out, or to draw a crowd.

And the woman is loud, persistent, not easily put off by being ignored. The disciples are fearful and want nothing to do with her, but they will not say anything to her. They nag Jesus and want him to get rid of her. In a sense they are heartless when they tell Jesus to send her away — or, in other words, "Make her shut up." Jesus says nothing in response to her cries. The woman is desperate and she is loud in describing her need — it's about her daughter, who is tormented by a demon. This can be any number of things: an illness, a fever, or something that causes her to have fits, lose control over her body. Or, as many exegetes think, it can be that the child is dying of slow starvation. The situation both in Israel and outside it was desperate in regard to having basic needs met. To feed their armies, the Romans took the harvest of everyone, both those occupying these territories and many others farther afield.[1] Many of the stories before and after this one have to do with food, with feeding large crowds and with faith or lack of it in the people. Jesus has just declared that any food that goes into a person is clean — it's the actions and words that come from a person that make it unclean. And in the previous chapter he has fed a crowd of "five thousand, not counting women and children" (Matt. 14:13-21). This is, in actuality, a huge number of people. The ratio of women and children to men in a crowd is about five or six to one. Even today when crowds are counted, the smallest number is counted loosely, and then the size of the crowd is extrapolated from that initial number. Based on these statistics, the group that Jesus fed was a crowd of 25,000 to 30,000 hungry people who, at the end of the story, were all "satisfied." And there was enough food left over to fill twelve wicker baskets — symbolically, enough for all of Israel.

The woman's cries to Jesus are direct, and she does not care about what his disciples or anyone else thinks. She calls him "Lord, Son of David," a title in Israel but not in her region or religion — whatever it is, Canaanite or Greek. And she wants his pity — her need is overwhelming — nothing else matters at all. The Greek translation of how she cries out is like the sound of a crow — cawing, annoying, loud, and never-ending. And Jesus, it seems, just ignores her, refusing to look at her or deign to answer her. When he talks to his disciples about their admonishment to get rid of her, his reason for not responding is an incredibly revelatory comment: "I was sent only to the lost sheep of the house of Israel." It is not about her except that he has nothing to do with her because of how he perceives himself, his identity, his mission, and his work: he is a prophet to the nation and the people of Israel, to the Jews only. But she doesn't care one whit what he thinks; she is determined to get him to respond to her, no matter what the response might be. What she does next will push boundaries, and she, who has already overstepped some bounds, will now break taboos, social mores, religious regulations, and standard, traditional practice among peoples, nations, religions, genders, and social classes.

> But the woman came and did him homage, saying, "Lord, help me." He said in reply, "It is not right to take the food of the children and throw it to the dogs." She said, "Please, Lord, for even the dogs eat the scraps that fall from the table of their masters." Then Jesus said to her in reply, "O woman, great is your faith! Let it be done for you as you wish." And her daughter was healed from that hour. (Matt. 15:25-28)

The language and repartee back and forth echoes the conversation between Buddha and the samurai in our earlier story! It is shocking, insulting, direct, the truth as each sees it in confrontation with the other. But the outcome is staggering for both parties. The woman moves beyond words to actions. The simple phrase "came and did him homage" in reality means that she came toward him on her hands and knees and grasped him around his ankles as one would a ruler or sovereign and pitifully pleaded, "Help me." Jesus is caught, trapped, and she is hanging onto him so that he cannot move, cannot escape her grasp. The disciples would have been horrified, as would anyone around them who had been summoned by her yelling out.

Finally, Jesus deigns to talk to her, and his words we find shocking, not conjuring any of the images of Jesus we often cling to — as compassionate, tender, sweet, obliging, and responding to everyone in need. This Jesus breaks all the stereotypes of easy caricature and is all too human for us. Everyone outside the covenant of Israel was considered untouchable, loathed, and despised. They were unclean (the subject of Jesus' immediately prior sermon), physically and religiously, in dogma, practice, and perception, and they were to be shunned lest one became unclean oneself by contact with them. Jesus' response about dogs (like pigs today) was a high insult. (Even today, the members of most Muslim communities consider all dogs unclean and cannot understand for a moment the West's treatment of dogs — often treated better than most human beings in the way they are fed, coddled, allowed to share the same bed and chair, be at the table and be given treats of food, delicacies by hand. For Muslims it is disgusting and demeaning, especially if one goes from that to attempting to touch another human being.) For us today, it would be the equivalent of Jesus saying to her, "It's not right to throw the food prepared for a feast out to the pigs in the sty." Jesus is referring to his words, his teachings, and his vision of the Holy One, the depth of intimacy his people are invited into with God and with one another by his Good News. But it seems that it only belongs to one group: the people of the First Covenant, the Jews.

But this woman is not to be put off by insults, intimidation, or retorts. She comes back with a dose of reality: Even the dogs under the table go for the scraps that fall, or what the children might toss away because they don't like it or want to eat it. She got Jesus dead to rights. And it is he who is utterly stunned and taken aback, and he does a total turnaround in an instant of insight, wisdom, and knowledge. The children he has been preaching to, traveling to, inviting into the kingdom of abiding peace based on justice, forgiveness, reconciliation, and mercy have been sitting at the table, taking what they want (which isn't much) and throwing the rest away. And she, in her need, will take the scraps, the leftovers, whatever they don't want.

If she is a dog in Jesus' eyes, that's just fine if that's what is necessary for him to notice her, hear her need, and respond, if he can or will, and help her child.

Her child is no different than any of the children of Israel — this is what she wants Jesus to see and to remember and take to heart when he is teaching and reaching out to people. It's either all children, all people, all nations — or it's not even the ones he's decided to bring his message to first. She calls him "Lord," and she will be his servant, on the ground, groveling and begging. She will acknowledge who he thinks he is: the Son of David, the son of the prophets, the son of the promises of the messiah to come — whatever. And she will cower at his feet and beg for what she needs — like a dog. In her humiliation, Jesus learns humility. In her desperation, Jesus learns something of faith. In her need and great love for her daughter, Jesus' own love is stretched beyond national and religious borders to become universal and intimately singular toward all. There is no one who is separated or denied the love of God, denied the dignity of being a human being and having what they need to survive, and there is no one who is not a bridge to the presence, the face of the Holy.

This moment is a benchmark in the Gospel of Matthew and a pivotal moment for Jesus. In a moment that is much like a koan in Buddhism, Jesus is enlightened by the words, the actions, and the presence of this woman — an outsider, a stranger, a foreigner, a despised enemy — and she is his teacher, his mentor, and his breath of the Spirit laying bare the truth. Religion, dogma, teachings, laws, rules — all are nothing if they do not make us more human and compassionate and able to see all peoples, all men, women, and children as images of God seeking to be known and revealed. If our religion and its practices and its adherents do not see everyone in this light, then it is no religion at all — it is a sham, a group one belongs to for security, for a sense of being better than others, and it is destructive and inhuman, not to mention irreligious. The word *religion* means to "tie or to bind together" like a sinew/muscle/bone and other organs are bound together at junctures and joints of movement that allow for viability and flexibility. Either our religion teaches us and forms us into bonding with all peoples, or it is not religion. No one is excluded from being human and being the face of God.

This is faith — and this woman has great faith. In an instant she becomes the model of a believer in the community of Matthew. And Jesus' words are her confirmation: "Let it be done for you as you wish." They are astounding words in the mouth of Jesus. (In Luke's Gospel, they are in Mary's mouth as words of assent and belief. Now they are directed to this unnamed woman by Jesus as he learns the depth and breadth of faithfulness!) And the power that now connects her and Jesus shoots out like electricity and heals her daughter. Her torment is over. What if, in this moment, at this time, Jesus is sharing sustenance with her and her child, just as he did before in Israel, when feeding the crowd, with the thousands sharing in his presence? We have to look at this in light of what follows:

> Moving on from there, Jesus walked by the Sea of Galilee, went up on the mountain, and sat down there. Great crowds came to him, having with them the lame, the blind, the deformed, the mute, and many others. They placed them at his feet, and he cured them. The crowds were amazed when they saw the mute speaking, the deformed made whole, the lame walking, and the blind able to see, and they glorified the God of Israel. (Matt. 15:29-31)

From this moment on, Jesus preaches hope, healing, forgiveness, reconciliation, peace based on justice, care of the poor, merciful connections, and sharing of food and resources to any and all who will listen and take it to heart, regardless of their country of origin, their nation, their caste/class, or their religion. And the message of how to be more human and more revelatory of God the Holy One begins to spread out into the whole world. This next paragraph in the story cements the covenant of God with all the earth: we are not to let sickness, hunger, deformity, blindness, muteness, or any other condition separate us from others — and so from the Holy One. The path of Jesus' life is altered, and now there are to be no boundaries, no peoples separated from sharing in what others have, no one excluded, and definitely no individual or any people hated, attacked, or otherwise treated as anything less than the beloved children of God, all seated at the one table and all looking like God!

This is a story of need: Jesus' need to change his mind and heart about who he thinks he is and what he is doing in his life, and the woman's need for her child to be released from torment, despair — for all and everything to be swept away that hinders human beings from living as God's beloved sons and daughters. She tells Jesus who he is! She stretches his mind and heart, calling him to constant conversion, so that he becomes more human with every moment and every encounter, learning more of the Truth that is larger than anyone yet is found in everyone. She speaks truth to power, and she can do so because she knows who she is — a mother of a child in need. She begs on behalf of another, in public, on her knees. She pushes Jesus out into the world, beyond his limits and borders, beyond the "lost sheep of the house of Israel" into the whole world as our house. She shares her need — pushes it in his face! — in her belief born of desperation, so that he can emerge from his cocoon into the larger awareness of who he is. And from this moment on, Jesus will look upon the whole world with compassion, calling himself "the Son of Man," belonging to all of history and all the world.

This is what we are to do for one another: dialogue and fill up what is lacking in each other. Community is born of shared needs and lacks. And the woman shares with Jesus her authority and truth born of those who suffer and cry out, especially on behalf of others. She has done for him what he could not do for himself. In the words of the book of Deuteronomy,

> Cut away, therefore, the thickening about your hearts and stiffen your necks no more. For the LORD your God is God supreme and Lord supreme, the great, the mighty, and the awesome God, who shows no favor and takes no bribe, but upholds the cause of the fatherless and the widow; and befriends the stranger, providing him with food and clothing. You too must befriend the stranger, for you were strangers in the land of Egypt. (Deut. 10:16-19, JSB)

If we see God, then, we are to act like our God and see others with the same eyes of God and treat them as our God has treated us. Each of us is meant to be a sanctuary for all others, a bridge to and from all others, disregarding barriers, boundaries, and breaches, reaching out, bending before others, and in dialogue with others. Sadly, many of us act more like the disciples — blind, deformed in their perceptions and actions, telling Jesus to make the woman go away, utterly without regard for those who are not "their own" people. This story can amply serve as a basis for how we are to approach one another, especially those we consider ourselves separate from, different from, and fearful of, and call our enemies.

64

In this encounter, those who are dominant and demanding and sure of themselves move toward being singular servants of all. Those who consider others irrelevant at best to their lives begin to become co-relational. The arrogant learn humility. Instead of dogma, there is dialogue. Those who are adamant about being the only or the primary source of truth and morality move toward being those who begin to come face to face with the necessity of tolerance and respect, knowing that others can teach them, reveal them to themselves, and preach to them as surely as they seek to call others to be converted. And in this moment we can see our own parochialism or nationalism or religion as blinkered, conceited, and self-righteous — and all of us needing to see the world and all its peoples as the sacrament of the Spirit of God, seeking constantly to reveal the presence and power of God among us. For Christians, the words of Petru Dumitriu can be a shocking reminder:

> Jesus Christ is always on the side of the crucified, and I believe he changes sides in the twinkling of an eye. He is not loyal to your group. He is loyal to the suffering.

This story in Matthew can invite us to look at the three religions of the Book and all the people of these religions in a new light — as those given to each other to learn more of God. There is a saying that has been attributed to all these religions: "Call God by whatever name you please. God's name is Truth." And our religion — especially if we claim belief and practice within the religions of Judaism, Christianity, and Islam — must make us sanctuaries for and bridges to each other in the world. We must relate to each other and all people as God's people and God's children. The message of all prophets in all religions must draw together the honor of God, the care of the poor, and the coming of justice, with no violence toward others.

We live limited lives until we "cross over" into the concrete world of another country, another culture, another tradition of worship. . . . I have left forever a small world to live with the tensions and the tender mercies of God's larger family.

Joan Puls, *Every Bush Is Burning*

There are three contemporary women, among many, I would like to single out: Hanan Ashrawi, a Palestinian Christian; Lynn Gottlieb, an American Jewish rabbi; and Shirin Ebadi, an Iranian Muslim. These women are intent on being prophets of the truth; interested in dialogue, peace-making, and being bridges back and forth between their people, their religious institutions, and their countries; steeped in their contemporary histories and places and yet dedicated in faith to hope, freedom, and living together in peace.

The first woman, Hanan Ashrawi, was born in the city of Nablus in the West Bank region of Tiberias in 1946, just two years before the formation of the state of Israel. This is the present-day site of the ancient story of the woman at the well in John 4. Ashrawi's family was relocated to Ramallah during the re-formation of the boundaries of Palestine, what the Palestinians, both Christians and Muslim Arabs, refer to as "Al Nakba" or "The Disaster." Her father, Daoud Mikhael, was one of the founders of the PLO, the Palestinian Liberation Organization, so she grew up in a climate of disruption, separation, violence, and struggle, and as a refugee, she was always searching for identity, place, and meaning in a history larger than any person or group. Her mother was an Anglican Episcopalian, and her father was Greek Orthodox; she sees herself as an Anglican. Both of her parents were faithfully dedicated to the human rights of all and the physical care and tending to the needs of all, no matter what their country of origin, their religion, or their language. In fact, her father was a doctor who influenced her and taught her how to live humanly, with dignity and a sense of herself, in difficult and dangerous circumstances and times. She speaks of him teaching her not to let her gender, her religion, her economic background, her nationality, or any other characteristic of life prevent her from living fully.

In an interview in *Sojourners* magazine with Rose Marie Berger, Ashrawi tells of her father's influence on her thinking and her relationships with others. She didn't know that her father had treated Jewish POWs when he was a doctor in British Mandate Palestine, and she returned home from studying in Beirut to find Jewish Israelis with her father, in their house. She lashed out:

"I said, 'What?! You are receiving Israelis in our house!' To me, at that time, it was traitorous. There was absolutely no fraternizing with the enemy and the occupiers." Her father invited her to hear what these Israeli Jews had to say. "They had come to thank my father for the way he treated them and for being so human and considerate to them in the midst of that war." She also learned that when her family had to escape from Tiberias, a Jewish doctor and friend of her father got them a truck. "My father kept saying there are no different values to human life. Human lives are equal. That has remained with me for a long time."[2]

Ashrawi is fierce in her commitment to her people and their right to their own land as Arabs, both Christian and Muslim. In 1991 she became the official spokesperson for the Palestinian delegation to the Middle East Peace Process in Madrid, where she debated and overwhelmed her Israeli counterpart, Benjamin Netanyahu (who would later become Israel's prime minister), on the issue of Palestinian independence. In this same interview, she reveals the core of her commitment and how she approaches both her own people and the rest of the world:

"Truth is not a popular commodity," stated Ashrawi. "The Palestinians tell me that even if what I say isn't happy or positive or what they want to hear, they respect the fact that I tell them the truth. I tell them the truth no matter how painful. Palestinians deserve the truth. And I believe [the] world needs to hear the truth. We need to challenge the prevailing version that is often quite erroneous, misleading, fabricated, and often racist when it comes to Palestinians."[3]

Ashrawi's dedication to the truth is coupled with a demand for compassion and justice for the plight of the Palestinian people, the majority of whom, she reminds us, just want to live in peace, with dignity and hope for their children and the freedom to practice their religion. She is aware of the simplistic divide of describing one group as all-corrupt and abusive of power, as democratic and protecting their right to their state no matter what it entails, and the other as terrorist and violent (within her own community). She recognizes this as destructive and continuing a situation where there can be little dialogue or a sense of the others as just human beings. She believes that she must work with certain groups in her own culture to broaden the base of the Palestinian cause for freedom and a homeland. So she works with the women, young people, the weak, and the disenfranchised so that there can be more of a possibility of meeting across borders and religious disagreements. She also underscores the absolute need for the cessation of violence, corruption, and lies on both sides as essential to any way forward. And because of this belief, she broke with Arafat in 1998 over corruption and his reluctance to share any leadership or democratic decision-making.

Ashrawi's truth is hard: the continual reminder of the cruelty and daily humiliations faced by the Palestinians throughout the occupied territory; the lack of basic necessities — access to clean water, decent food, medical services (just continuation of medicines and treatments), and safe, clean places to deliver babies and provide for new mothers and children as well as the elderly and infirm. She believes that any change must begin with commiseration — appreciation for the traumatic suffering being experienced by an entire people, generations that know only deprivation, imprisonment in their land, constant violence, and insults to who they are as the Palestinian people living under a brutal army that for the most part does not see them or treat them as fellow human beings.

In the late 1990s, Ashrawi founded an independent human rights organization, The Palestinian Initiative for the Promotion of Global Dialogue and Democracy (MIFTAH), and she now travels extensively, seeking to educate groups on the reality of what it is like to live in Palestine, the history and politics of the Middle East, and how crucial it is to find a process of peace with abiding justice for all. She sees Palestine as the linchpin or key to the Middle East and much that must happen to draw the Arab and the Western world together, and the Muslim, Christian, and Israeli peoples together; how the United States and other Western countries treat Palestine is the revelatory core of what can and must change for all in the region. She states clearly, "People do not understand that the key to the stability and peace of the region

68

is Palestine. They do not understand that the U.S. has always been measured, in terms of its standing and integrity, by how it treats the Palestinians."[4]

Ashrawi's suggestions for what others can do? "Caritas. Charity. Show us basic human compassion in our suffering. Bear witness and speak out." These are words that echo the ones her father would repeat to her when she was young. And she suggests that people show solidarity and accompaniment by visiting Palestine to observe, support, work with, educate, and offer their presence, unarmed and vulnerable, to the people who struggle so to stay and live there. It has and is and probably will be a long struggle ahead, and there is still a great need to cry out on behalf of others — on behalf of the children and those who have known only slow starvation, violence, terror, and humiliation at the hands of others. Ashrawi often ends her talks by referring to a time when Palestinians protested against Israeli tanks and guns by walking up to them and putting olive branches into the gaping openings. "We can do that again," she says, "but they have to stop shooting at us first." She is adamant about the need for what she calls "proactive, intrusive, and nonviolent resistance, even as a largely defenseless population."[5]

Prayer at the Kindling of Light
Blessed be she who kindles the flames of creation.
Blessed be he who sparks the imagination.
Blessed be those who weave threads of light throughout
the generations,
Who turn our longing for peace into illumination.

Lynn Gottlieb, *She Who Dwells Within*[6]

Another remarkable woman is Rabbi Lynn Gottlieb, an American who has worked with the Fellowship of Reconciliation as a Middle East Program Associate with the American Friends Service Committee in San Francisco, and is the recent cofounder of Shomer Shalom Institute for Jewish Non-Violence. With these organizations and communities she travels often to the Middle East — to Israel, to Iran, to Gaza in Palestine, and to other Arab lands — seeking to humanize the face of Israel and the Jewish communities in all these places. The *Jewish Post* has described her as a pioneering female rabbi who was one of the first ten women in Jewish history to enter rabbinic life, and who in 1980 was ordained in the Jewish Renewal Movement. She has served as the sole rabbi to Temple Beth Or of the Deaf and the Hebrew Association of the Deaf. She studied at Hebrew Union College and at the Jewish Theological Seminary, and with great teachers such as Rabbi Zalman Schacter, Everett Gendler, Wolfe Kelman, and Elie Wiesel. This is how the Jewish community describes her:

> While most of the Jewish community was focused on equal access, Lynn was engaged in "the transformation of Judaism itself." During the next decade [1970-80], Lynn helped forge what has now become the Jewish Renewal Movement by pioneering a nonsexist, ecologically responsible Jewish peace culture with a special focus on creativity and the arts. By 1977, Lynn had become a "teacher and a spiritual guide . . . to thousands of American Jews . . . and led them to reclaim their Jewish heritage, to discover the divine presence, and perhaps, for the first time in their life, to feel at home in the Jewish community."[7]

From 1982 until 2000, Gottlieb was the founding rabbi for the Congregation Nahalat Shalom in Albuquerque, New Mexico. She is a scholar, a peace advocate working for human rights, a performing artist — puppeteer, storyteller, and singer — and passionately dedicated to Jewish spirituality, inclusion, and communion. Susannah Heschel has noted, "Lynn Gottlieb's remarkable insight into the spiritual dimensions of Judaism brings out religious meaning that speaks to every person of faith." And that is the core of this woman's work, hope, and faith.

Gottlieb's travels to Gaza and Iran especially give her a unique vantage point. It allows her to critique and encourage her own people in the Jewish community who are struggling for a way to live in peace with their neighbors in Palestine and with many in the Middle East. It also allows her to give courage and hope to the Palestinians and to those Muslims seeking alternatives to existing violent realities within their own communities and dialogue with Israel and the Western world.

In 2008 she wrote a letter to her friends (posted on her Web site) in honor of Hanukkah, reminding her own people of the history and depth of spiritual meaning behind their celebrations and how that meaning must be interpreted today in relation to Gaza and the militant attacks against the Palestinians. The entire letter is stunning in its breadth of scholarship and history and its depth of perception of the impact that spirituality and ritual can have on a community and current affairs. Here are a few short portions of what she preaches, exhorts, begs, and sings about as part of her tradition:

Dear Friends . . . Let us call for an immediate end to the siege of Gaza, an end to the firing of rockets into Israel, and an immediate return to the ceasefire. And then, let us call for meaningful negotiations that result in concrete advances toward peace based on mutual recognition, systematic equality, and good-neighbor policies in the land that both people share.

For those who justify defensive violence on the basis of the Maccabean struggle in 165 BCE that resulted in taking back the Temple in Jerusalem, I believe that then, as now, militarism is a fatal mistake and does not bring lasting or temporary peace. Roger Kamenitz once commented: "If one is compassionate, then one has a compassionate Torah. If one is angry, one's Torah is also angry." All the more so if one believes that violence can ever be redemptive.

. . . Great is peace. . . . I believe the message of Torah and Talmud counsels us to embrace the miracle of peace rather than place our faith in the sword. That is, I believe, also the message of Hanukkah given to us by the sages. The Talmudic sages did not spend too much time on the Maccabean victory. One sentence. After all, the Temple was destroyed by the Romans in 70 CE. The people of Israel two thousand years ago were living under Roman occupation. Rather, the people and the sages emphasized a story about the miracle of the oil and proposed a new ceremonial way to proclaim continuity and hope: lighting a hanukkah in the window at dusk to proclaim the miracle of light in a time of darkness. Lighting candles was their form of resistance to death and persecution. It worked. We survived.

. . . Violence is rooted in fear and despair as well as the ability to act without restraint. Let us embrace the miracle of hope and peace by calling for an immediate ceasefire and an end to the siege of Gaza. Let us be the voice of restraint. Make it a public witness. Place your faith in acts of peace. Do not be silent in the face of violence. Let your voice be another candle in the darkness.[8]

Gottlieb visited Iran five times in 2008 and 2009, attending services in Shiraz and Teheran and having conversations for hours on end with the Jewish communities there and with scholars, youth, elders, and many non-Jews.

The Jewish community in Iran is between 30,000 and 40,000 people, the oldest Jewish community in the Middle East — three thousand years old in one place! Here is a vivid description of them:

They are rooted in the land of Cyrus. They can visit the graves of Esther and Mordecai, Daniel and Habakkuk. They possess a Torah that is over 1200 years old. . . . The Jews of Iran are deeply proud of their own heritage, even though they, like other Iranians, may struggle with the limitations imposed by the Islamic republic on freedom of expression.[9]

Gottlieb spoke out in response to Hillary Clinton's statement that "an Iranian assault on Israel would be met with an American response that would 'obliterate' Iran." She responded in turn, saying,

It is important to negotiate and not threaten obliteration, in particular because there are between 30,000 and 40,000 Jewish people living in Iran. Our mission, the fifth such one, is one of friendship and solidarity to Iran of the New York-based Fellowship of Reconciliation (FOR) and is coordinated on the Iranian side with the Iranian Center for Interfaith Dialogue, described by FOR as "an official entity committed to supporting interaction between different religious communities."[10]

She further describes these delegations and visitors that do meet with government officials but notes that "our purpose [is] to meet civilian groups in the religious community, in arts and culture, students, women's groups." It's all part of an effort at "civilian diplomacy," which Gottlieb describes as "people-to-people [connections] to create a more positive environment on the ground for people to exchange productive dialogue and to create more understanding, to humanize the face of the enemy on both sides."[11]

Gottlieb's views are strong and pointed, telling the truth to Israeli, Palestinian, and Arab societies, as well as to U.S. and other Western societies. When asked about Iran as a threat to Israel, she gave this reply:

> I don't think Iran is going to attack Israel: I think it's a chimera. Iran has never initiated a war. And the fact that Israel has never signed the nuclear Non-Proliferation Treaty, and that it has nuclear weapons, is one of the reasons why Iran wants nuclear weapons. Israel has already bombed Iraq and Syria. It is not [unreasonable] for Iran to think it will also be a target. Maybe we should be pressuring everybody to sign the NPT. We should be [backing] the forces of peace, not the forces advocating war. . . . I think the American public accepts certain conventional ideas which are not borne out in history. For instance, in the last 50 years there have been 72 nonviolent revolutions all around the world. If you ask the Iranian people, they are pleading with us not to go to war, saying to us, "Let us solve our own problems, and let us work in our societies to make the changes we desire."[12]

In 2008, Gottlieb was one of a handful of Jews and the only rabbi to attend a dinner dialogue between Ahmadinejad and a coalition of religious peace groups at the United Nations. It was eerily quiet as she stood to speak, and she was well aware that whatever she would say would be met with both criticism and hope. She said she was careful, not wanting to insult Ahmadinejad but wanting to keep channels open. She cited the first passage in Leviticus, which commands, "Do not . . . spread hate among peoples." She continued, "Hate speech is to be avoided because it often leads to acts of violence. As you are well aware, I come from a community that has experienced the genocidal results of hate speech leading to hate action." She spoke of mourning her own Jewish family in the Holocaust, and the mass murder of two million Armenians, one million Roma, and tens of thousands who died on account of sexual orientation as well as those who were targeted for murder based on special needs. And she said she learned from the rabbis who ordained her "to be active in preventing further suffering of all human beings," specifically saying, "I, like thousands of Jewish Americans, Israelis, and Europeans, have joined with other peace activists across the globe to work tirelessly for Palestinian human rights, an end to anti-Semitism, as well as Israeli-Palestinian reconciliation through the path of non-violence." She was the first, and all who followed her sought to confront him, demanding responses from him and challenging him. It was a diplomatic event, but also another opportunity to speak the truth and seek a conversation of openness and hope.[13]

Here are Gottlieb's words as she ended that trip, planned for another, and also planned to attend the Founders Conference of Shomer Shalom in Chicago in 2008. They sum up her constant daily devotion and what she hopes for and how to achieve it for all:

> I'm hoping to create a movement of Jewish people to study nonviolence both as a strategy and as a way of life, to create seeds of peace, to build and nourish peace and understanding. That's what we're called to do in our tradition. I'm fulfilling a mitzvah, and that's what a rabbi is supposed to do.
>
> I am not naïve — I've been at this for a long time, and I'm a student of history. . . . I simply have great faith in the goodness of people, and I want to encourage that. I don't want to sit back passively while violence increases.
>
> I am expecting to face criticism for this trip, but criticism can't stop us from thinking generations ahead. I'm doing this for my children and my grandchildren.[14]

We suffer from an incurable malady: Hope.
                                        Mahmoud Darwish, Palestinian poet

The third woman in this trinity is Shirin Ebadi, often called Iran's troublemaker, in the tradition of Elijah the prophet, also referred to by this name by the king of Israel. She is new to the public scene — meaning outside of her native Iran. Stuart Jeffries interviewed her for the "Weekly Review" of the *Guardian Weekly,* and he describes her this way: "She has lived through three eras in Iran: the monarchy, the Islamic republic, and the current, confrontational regime, and been a thorn in the side of all three."[15]

Ebadi has won the Nobel Peace Prize and has written a memoir entitled *Iran Awakening: A Memoir of Revolution and Hope.*[16] She has known the usual humiliations of being treated like a child by authorities and police, needing permission from her husband or mother to do certain things — at the age of forty-five! She has also known repression, oppression, insult, inequality, and injustice. Under Islamic law, the testimony of two women is equal to that of one man, and a man can divorce his wife without any good reason, while it is nearly impossible for a woman to divorce her husband. Ebadi tells of worse things still in her memoir: of murder threats, time spent in jail, and the harassment that she, her husband, and her daughters have had to endure because she speaks out in public as a human rights defender and a relentless advocate for women and those caught in the struggle for dignity and equality in her country. She lives with the threat of assassination, and with the reality that since she has left Iran, she probably will not be allowed to return.

Even after receiving the Nobel Prize in 2003, her life has not improved. Since she is more public, she is attacked by the government and its leaders more often. They sought to degrade her winning of the prize by saying that it was a political gesture and not important. Ebadi proved them wrong: she took the prize money, deposited it in a bank, and used it to help prisoners of conscience and their families (attested to by a founding member of Ebadi's human rights group, Muhammad Ali Dadkhah). Ebadi did leave Iran shortly before the elections, which saw Mahmoud Ahmadinejad return to office in 2009. These elections were accompanied by human rights abuses and massive protests from hundreds of thousands of Iranian students and people from all levels of society. Since then, Iranian officials have blocked her husband's bank accounts, illegally frozen her accounts, and confiscated her Nobel Prize medal, criticizing her even more in public. They say that she owes taxes on the prize money — though under Iranian law, it should not be taxed. The move is meant to keep Ebadi from returning to Iran; if she does, she will be arrested under the pretext of tax evasion. This is seen as part of a planned increase of pressure on human rights advocates and anyone who dissents or attempts to offer lawful criticism of the government.

Given these events, it is interesting to learn that Ebadi was born in Iran in 1947 to parents who treated her as equal to her brother and sent her to college. At the age of twenty-three, she became Iran's first woman judge. She believes that the beginning of any revolution or change or real transformation begins with the education of women. In her book she writes, "Allowing women into higher education (while the Taliban in Afghanistan forbade women to read) instilled something in Iranian women that will, in the long run, I believe, transform Iran: a visceral consciousness of their oppression."[17] Strangely enough, as Iran shifted from a monarchy to the Islamic republic under Ayatollah Khomeini in 1979, Ebadi was removed as a judge. Paradoxically, she became the secretary of the same court that she once presided over. She was informed that Islam forbids women judges. Again, as part of this paradox, Ebadi had initially supported the revolution that had overthrown the Shah, hoping for more democracy under Khomeini. But within a few years, the situation had so devolved that she was on a death list, jailed, and put in solitary confinement.

And yet Ebadi loves Iran. When asked why she has stayed most of her life, how she can bear the reprisals, and what has happened over the years to undo what little freedoms that existed earlier in her life, she is clear about why she has remained:

> I am an Iranian. I must live in Iran. If someone has got a mother who is very old or ill, do they leave them in the street to die, or do they take her home until she recovers? I feel my country is ailing in the same way.[18]

Although removed as judge and denied the access to practice law, she once again established a pro-bono law practice from the early 1990s on, specifically choosing cases that would expose injustice and human rights abuses in the revolutionary legal system. She has dealt with rape, child abuse, murder, blood feuds, cases of enforcing blood money provisions for criminal punishments — and many other abuses unique to Iran. The Nobel Prize gave her publicity outside Iran and a platform to speak out more universally, to defend Islamic law and religion and yet recognize the diversity in interpretation in various countries and groups within Islam. She is dedicated to Iranian democracy. In her book's epilogue, she writes,

> The Iranian revolution has produced its own opposition, not least a nation of educated, conscious women who are agitating for their rights. They must be given the chance to fight their own fights, to transform their country uninterrupted.[19]

She is committed to freedom, democracy, and independence for her country, the practice of the law in Iran, and law in the Islamic religious traditions. She once told an interviewer, "Fear is an instinct, like hunger, and we all know it. I have learned not to let fear prevent me from doing what I should do." She said her faith was still strong. "I am against patriarchy, not Islam." And she continued: "Islam, like any other religion, has different interpretations. . . . In Saudi Arabia women can't even drive; in Indonesia, Bangladesh, and Pakistan, they have been political leaders." She believes that Islam is a religion of peace and equality for all.[20]

As of this writing, Shirin Ebadi has not yet returned to Iran.

These three women show the power of dialogue, hope, and the cry for justice on behalf of others — their children and grandchildren, others' children, those who have known persecution, injustice, and diminished life because of religion and politics. Each in her own way cries out and will not be silenced. Each brings insight and understanding, wisdom and interpretation of reality that are desperately needed by others — whoever the "others" are in this world. They survive. They endure. They are faithful. They must live on the hope that Simone Weil once wrote about, even if they have never read her words: "Even if our efforts of attention seem for years to be producing no result, one

day a light that is in exact proportion to them will flood the soul."
And it is hoped that this light will flood the world around them where
they seek to be bridges for others to walk across and meet.

Sources Used in This Chapter

Shirin Ebadi. *Iran Awakening.* London: Rider, 2006.

Lynn Gottlieb. *She Who Dwells Within: A Feminist Vision of a Renewed Juda-ism.* San Francisco: Harper, 1995.

Hagar, Sarah, and Their Children: Jewish, Christian, and Muslim Perspectives. Edited by Phyllis Trible and Letty M. Russell. Louisville: Westminster John Knox Press, 2006.

Praise Her Works: Conversations with Biblical Women. Edited by Penina Adelman. Philadelphia: Jewish Publication Society, 2005.

Ziauddin Sardar and Merryl Wyn Davies. *The No-Nonsense Guide to Islam.* Oxford, U.K.: New Internationalist Publications, 2004.

Turning Wheel, Fall/Winter 2009, the issue dedicated to Israel/Palestine, Iran, etc. See specifically a long article by Alice Walker, "Overcoming Speechlessness: A Poet Encounters the 'Horrors' of Rwanda, Eastern Congo, and Palestine/Israel," pp. 12-26. See the Buddhist Peace Fellowship site, www.bpf.org.

Chapter 5

Food and Land

The world is holy. We are holy. All life is holy. Daily prayers are delivered on the lips of breaking waves, the whisperings of grasses, the shimmering of leaves.

Terry Tempest Williams

We are born hungry, crying out for nourishment, for touch and presence. We use words like *hunger* and *consuming* to speak of deeper longings, primeval needs: for friendship, acceptance, love, dignity, knowledge, power. In some ways we are known by our hungers and hopes, and our societies are characterized by what consumes us and drives us. Hunger can draw us beyond our bodies, beyond our rational minds, beyond what usually fills the soul, into what is inexhaustible, eternal, and mysteriously fully human, bordering on the divine. But hunger can also eat us alive, reduce us to being imprisoned in our bodies where sleep, movement, and all thoughts revolve around the next time we will have food to eat. Hunger can be a devouring addiction. Originally, the word *consumption* referred to a disease; now it is an economic and personal characteristic of our culture. We are often referred to as "consumers." In the last one hundred years, we have devoured so much of the earth and its resources that we are stealing food and sustenance out of the mouths of our children and grandchildren, while we live without any compunction about the gulfs between those who are rich and those who are poor. The United Nations defines the rich as "those who have more than enough to survive on today." That defines many of us. And yet, the U.N. Food and Agriculture Organization reported recently that the number of hungry and undernourished people in the world reached an all-time high of 1.02 billion people, about 100 million more than in 2008. That's about 1 in 6 people in the world, or 15 percent of the global population.

The issues of hunger and food are intimately connected to the issues of land, farming, and climate change that aggravates and intensifies these realities. For more than 70 percent of the people of the world, agriculture and land are fundamentally important: subsistence farming is their primary means of survival. The connections between food and land and farming and religion are moral and ethical realities that impact ritual and worship. And still, so many go underfed or unfed — a sad reality in a world that claims to be spiritually mature and where the major religions all proclaim the importance of pursuing justice, caring for the poor and the neediest, avoiding waste and excess, sharing one's possessions, and serving and preserving the earth's resources of land, water, and food.

When Gandhi spoke of Christians and their ritual of the breaking and sharing of the bread, he commented, "Your God was wise — he stayed among you as bread. If God had been Indian, he would have stayed as rice." The earth, the land we dwell on, is God's original sanctuary, and how we handle the element of bread (the symbol, like rice or corn/maize, of sustenance) and the element of wine (the symbol, like water and milk, of feasting and celebrating) is more revelatory of our worship of God and the state of relationships within our communities than what happens in any other ritual of church worship. We sing the ancient psalm line over and over: "Taste and see, taste and see, taste and see the goodness of the Lord." But oftentimes we do so without gratitude, without sharing it with others, and without giving thought to what is left over or wasted.

I will never ever forget being in Haiti and the Dominican Republic years ago, walking along one of the dirt roads, so thirsty, sipping water from a bottle I carried and chewing on a health-food bar that had the consistency of straw, and thinking to myself how awful it was. I had no sooner finished my fortified energy snack when I passed a woman with a baby on her back, about five or six months' pregnant, on her hands and knees along the side of the road. To my horror, I realized that she was collecting mud and making it into a small pie, patting it and spitting into it to hold it together. Then she sat in the grass and began eating it slowly. When I sat down with her and began talking with her, she told me that she was very careful about what dirt she ate — only dirt that was in a field, off the roads where people traveled and animals defecated. She wanted to be very careful since she was pregnant. I had heard stories about this gruesome reality, but seeing it broke open a place in me where rage could flourish. I gave her my other three energy bars, telling her that they were nutritional and would be good for her and the baby — the one on her back — if she could break it up so the baby could teethe on it. She smiled with such light and gratitude that I wept all the way back to where I was staying. Since then I have read that mudcakes — made of mud, salt, shortening, and sugar, or some mixture of these — have gone up steeply in price, and the hungry can't even afford them. They have acquired a name: pica.

In all the Gospels we find the story of mass feedings by Jesus. There are slight variations in the stories, but they all focus on the basics of survival: bread and a bit of extra protein — fish. (Interestingly, the early Christians often signed the places where they gathered with the word ICHTHUS; it means "fish" and is also an anagram of Jesus Christ, Son of God, the Savior.) The other focus is on who eats, how many eat, and how the feeding process is organized.

The account from John has a few details added that are important to our topics of food and land. Jesus is finding that many in a crowd that he's telling the good news refuse to believe his words, so he leaves and crosses the Sea of Tiberias. (The Jews lived always under the eye of Rome, which appropriated all the food/crops of the fertile northern areas, leaving the people hungry and begging, suffering from malnourishment and slow starvation.) Jesus then goes up a mountain and sits down with his disciples. (We are told that it's close to the Feast of Passover, the feast of freedom from slavery, hunger, and oppression. It is celebrated with ritual foods in memory of bitterness, hardship, freedom, escape from bondage, and salvation from death — among them

the lamb sacrificed by families in the temple and shared standing at
the table.) The crowd has followed him across the sea, and now they
assemble around him, because they have seen and heard what he is
doing with those who are sick and in need.

> When Jesus raised his eyes and saw that a huge crowd was coming
> to him, he said to Philip, "Where can we buy enough food for them
> to eat?" He said this to test him, because he himself knew what he
> was going to do. Philip answered him, "Two hundred days wages'
> worth of food would not be enough for each of them to have a little
> [bit]." One of his disciples, Andrew, the brother of Simon Peter, said
> to him, "There is a boy here who has five barley loaves and two fish;
> but what good are these for so many?" Jesus said, "Have the people
> recline." Now there was a great deal of grass in that place. So the
> men reclined, about five thousand in number. (John 6:5-10)

The stage is carefully set. Jesus is the one to initiate the work of pro-
viding food and feeding the crowd, and he engages his disciples in the
work — questioning them and seeing what they think of the situation.
Basically, Philip's answer is one of helplessness: he feels overwhelmed
with the immensity of the task, and how much it will cost to give
them just one meal — two hundred days' wages — about two-thirds of
a year's work for one person fully employed. Andrew offers a bit of information: he knows a young boy (younger than twelve, still to celebrate his bar mitzvah). He has five barley loaves and two fish — but
what good is so little among so many? (Barley loaves are the food of
the poor. A barley loaf is coarse, heavy, and stays in one's stomach longer, offering some relief from hunger pangs. In biblical times the
loaves were usually round and weighed one to three pounds each.)[1]
But Jesus knows what to do. And he does the community organizing
— getting the people seated on the grass, even telling them to recline
— in effect saying, "Rest, and prepare to eat." It seems John's feeding
story is definitely a picnic!

> Then Jesus took the loaves, gave thanks, and distributed them to
> those who were reclining, and also as much of the fish as they

wanted. When they had had their fill, he said to his disciples, "Gather the fragments left over, so that nothing will be wasted." So they collected them, and filled twelve wicker baskets with fragments from the five barley loaves that had been more than they could eat. When the people saw the sign he had done, they said, "This is truly the Prophet, the one who is to come into the world." (John 6:11-14)

And there are two other details of great importance. About five thousand men are in the crowd. No mention is made of women and children, but sociologists who use statistics to count crowds would estimate the ratio of women and children to men to be about five or six to one. So this is a new exodus, a new people sharing food, set free and becoming a people as they eat together. And one wonders about the boy. Did his mother send him with the food? It is the women who would have carried the food as they followed Jesus to the other side of the lake, and the men would have carried the sick on pallets. Was she related to Andrew? Was she Peter's mother-in-law? One can wonder.

And Jesus models what is to be done: he takes the loaves and fishes, gives thanks, and distributes them to the people. It sounds simple enough. The Jewish people refer to the Scriptures as black fire on white fire, and teach that there is as much told and revealed in the white fire — the page — as there is in the black fire: the text itself. What is the sign? What is the miracle? Many communities flesh out this passage. They say that the crowd of women, children, and men watched Jesus take the loaves and fishes from the young boy and give the food to them, and they in turn reached into their garments and bags and took out what they were carrying: loaves, fish, dates, figs, wineskins — traveling food — the equivalent of my water bottle and health-food bar. Those not counted — the majority of the people — were the ones that prepared the food and distributed it. So, in imitation of Jesus, they shared their supplies with everyone else — as the young boy did with Jesus. And there is enough — in fact, everyone has enough, and there is so much left over! And then Jesus commands his disciples to get up and collect the leftovers — there is to be no waste. The excess is to be collected and shared just as the main meal was shared with those there. And even the baskets full of food — twelve of them, symbolic of all the tribes of the land — come from the crowd's gifting and sharing. The sign is that of justice — food for all, the possibility of life for all, especially those not counted or considered of equal value to others in an economy/work/profit-driven society that lived under oppression and in slavery on their own land.

It seems that Jesus believed in what is today referred to as "food sovereignty" as the prophetic demand for care of the poor. A recent report from the G8 summit meeting in Japan states what this means pragmatically:

> It would mean taking food and agriculture policy out of trade and international financial institution agreements and putting it into the hands of people who produce and need food. . . .[2]

And the report describes "food sovereignty" this way:

> Food sovereignty is the right of peoples to healthy and culturally appropriate food produced through ecologically sound and sustainable methods, and their right to define their own food and agriculture systems. It puts the aspirations and needs of those who produce, distribute, and consume food at the heart of food policies rather than markets and corporations.[3]

This is the miracle that is needed, the sign of the times now in the world. The miracle of a world free from hunger depends on the human community and its belief in the necessity of sharing and changing the ways it deals with excess and waste. There were twelve wicker baskets — good-sized ones — left over after Jesus' picnic. Who went home with them? Who was fed after the picnic was over, the crowd dispersed, and everyone went back to their places — fields, farms, villages, cities? These are the issues that the world is dealing with today. What we do with our discarded bread will be part of what we are held accountable for and judged upon. The production, storage, transportation, and packaging of our food produces massive amounts of waste, especially when so much is just thrown out and not eaten. If we stop wasting food that could be eaten, we could feed eighty million people a day!

It is interesting that the word *economics* comes from the root word *oikos* (Greek), which also means "household." Economics, especially in regard to food, land, and excess/waste, has social functions. A healthy economics reveals social equality as the norm, enhances people's lives and the human infrastructures that strengthen society, and teaches social responsibility. An unhealthy economics reveals inequality and disregard for human beings and resources, insults creation and the God of all things and peoples, and reveals what in our value systems need immediate conversion and altered priorities. People must come first; next, land and resources (evenly weighted as much as possible); next, just and creative ways of dealing with waste; and only then profit. Good economic practice in regard to food, land, and resources commits itself to the well-being of God's entire household, beginning with those most in need and the majority: the poor, children, women of child-bearing age, the sick, and those without ties to a community for support. Even the word *budget* comes from the original idea of a bag or a sack, and what we do with the contents of what we can carry — limited resources that call for imaginative structures and action. What specifically is called for? Workable groups — farm and food co-ops, base communities, community gardeners, neighborhood alliances, parishes, and church coalitions — bioregions, biospheres, local produce and local consumption, control of land and water rights, communal property rather than corporately controlled property, and responses that deal with both immediate daily needs as well as long-term needs that remember those who come after us — down to the seventh generation.

There are two women, both by the name of Dorothy, who are already remembered for how they dealt with hungry people, food, the land, and food-and-land sovereignty: Dorothy Day and Dorothy Mae Stang. Here are words from Dorothy Day that draw many of these pieces together:

We cannot love God unless we love each other. We know him in the breaking of the bread, and we know each other in the breaking of the bread, and we are not alone anymore. Heaven is a banquet, and

85

life is a banquet too — even with a crust — where there is companionship. We have all known loneliness, and we have learned that the only solution is love, and that love comes with community.[4]

Dorothy Day is best known as the author of books such as *The Long Loneliness* and as the founder, along with Peter Maurin, of the Catholic Worker movement in 1933, more than seventy-five years ago. This movement spawned the *Catholic Worker* newspaper — then a soup kitchen, a farming commune, and a house of hospitality for the homeless, where there were regular Friday-night lectures on every relevant topic imaginable: issues in the Catholic Church, communism, economics, the draft, resistance to war, nonviolence, justice, prayer, and peace, among others. Day was about as down-to-earth as could be imagined, fiery, passionate, devoted to the poor and to community and to the corporal works of mercy as a lifestyle. She was able to poke fun at herself and be withering in regards to others. She could be demanding and playful. She loved opera, a good glass of wine (and smoking), books, and praying. Her story is a remarkable journey of a an American woman — a writer, a communist, and a convert to Catholicism (what she called the "belief of the masses") in 1927. She was serious about praying, and equally serious about resisting violence, the draft, war, nuclear weapons, and power. She was a person of many paradoxes and could carry within herself a number of ambiguities better than others could. In an interview with the *Catholic Agitator*, Dan McKanan (author of *The Catholic Worker after Dorothy: Practicing the Works of Mercy in a New Generation*) talks about Dorothy's idea of the Catholic Worker, but more about the underlying works of mercy that sourced every aspect of her life:

> The Catholic Worker has never held that the only way to live out the works of mercy is in the context of a large urban hospitality house that the movement is best known for, or indeed that this is even the best place to live them. "We always have more to feed and house and to clothe than we can humanly handle," Dorothy critiqued her own house in New York. "Breadlines are a disgrace." Meeting and knowing Christ in the poor, living in solidarity with the poor, and serving at a personal sacrifice can be done in many

ways. The "Christ room" that St. John Chrysostom suggested that every family provide for a stranger in need has often been cited by Dorothy as an ideal: "We must never cease emphasizing the fact that the work must be kept small."[5]

McKanan continues connecting Dorothy's ideas about corporal and spiritual works of mercy in practice and life:

> As a hermeneutical principle, the works of mercy help account for the extraordinary depth of the Catholic Worker movement. The practice of the works of mercy must be interpreted more broadly than simply providing direct service to those in need. The one time that Dorothy Day mentioned me in her "On Pilgrimage" column was when I was arrested with a group blocking rail shipment of plutonium into a nuclear weapons factory. "I rejoice to see the young people thinking of 'the works of mercy' as a truly revolutionary, but nonviolent program. The spiritual and corporal certainly go together," she wrote, "and often involve suffering."[6]

Perhaps one of the more amazing things about Dorothy's life was how she wove together her personal life, her family life, and her public work and persona. Born in 1897, she grew up in Chicago, knowing the Depression era. She went to college and became active as a Communist, then began writing for *The Call* and *The Masses*. During this time she was married, divorced, and had an abortion. She was also jailed with other suffragettes who protested outside the White House. She fell deeply in love with Foster Batterham and had their child, Tamar, in 1926. It was at this point that she felt strongly led to the Catholic faith. When she baptized Tamar and was baptized herself, Batterham left her. Despite this loss, McKanan says that "she always believed that it was possible to combine family life with the works of mercy."[7] And today, thirty years after Dorothy's death, the 185 Catholic Worker houses — many of which raise families — are flourishing. In fact, many of the communities are more than twenty-five years old and have seen generations of worker families.

Day was known for her "radical" politics (meaning that they were deeply rooted in the Scriptures and the early church) and was as pious a believer in her time as one might find — if by "pious" one means being devoted and prayerful, reflecting on the Scriptures with others, and reading everyone from St. Therese (the Little Flower) to Jacques Maritain, G. K. Chesterton, Leon Bloy, Étienne Gilson, C. S. Lewis, D. H. Lawrence, and Ignazio Silone. She loved music — Bach, Brahms, and opera — and she loved her friends — Daniel Berrigan, Flannery O'Connor, Thomas Merton, Joan Baez, Eileen Egan, Mother Teresa, Peter Maurin, Ade Bethune, Tom Cornell, Robert Ellsberg, Catherine De Hueck Doherty, and so many others. And she was a good friend. In fact, when Foster Batterham's longtime companion, Nanette, fell ill with cancer, she asked Dorothy to take care of her — and she did.

In 1973, while picketing with the United Farm Workers in Palo Alto, California, Day was arrested for the last time. Shortly before that, she had spoken at the Joan Baez Institute for the Study of Nonviolence. Robert Ellsberg, who published Day's diaries, quotes the last line of this speech and gives a memorable description of her:

> "The true anarchist asks nothing for himself. He is self-disciplined, self-denying, accepting the Cross, without asking sympathy, without complaint." Her words could have been a caption for the famous photo of that day in Delano: mouth set, eyes fierce, staring down an armed policeman.[8]

And yet the story about Dorothy Day that I love best comes even later, toward the end of her life, when she went with others from the New York house to a protest. She was sitting in a small, fold-up canvas chair. She had her glasses on and her hair pulled back in braids, and she was wearing a straw hat — it was a hot day. She was approached by one of the New York policemen — who knew her by sight — and he said to her, "Miss Day, what are you doing here at your age? What are you protesting now?"

Day, sometimes a bit forgetful of details at that point, responded, "You know, officer, I'm not exactly sure — but you can ask any of these young people, and they'll tell you what we're here for. They are very reliable and very truthful." Needless to say, the policeman, one of New

York's finest, was at first stunned by her answer, then laughed out loud. He patted her on the head and told her to take good care of herself.

Here are a few memorable lines from Day, culled from the one-liners in my own collection and that of my friend John Dear:

> Poverty is a strange and elusive thing. I have tried to write about it, its joys and its sorrows, for thirty years now. I condemn poverty, and I advocate it. Poverty is simple and complex at once: it is a social phenomenon and a personal matter.

> Someone asked her once, "How long do you let the poor stay?" She answered, "We let them stay forever. They live with us, they die with us, and we give them a Christian burial. . . . They become members of the family. Or rather, they always were members of the family. They are our brothers and sisters in Christ."

> Those who can't see Christ in the poor are atheists indeed.

> Becoming a saint is the revolution.

> Once you give to God what is God's, there's nothing left for Caesar.

> Love is a great and holy force and must be used as a spiritual weapon.

> *You must turn to God like the sunflowers always turn to the sun.*
> *St. Julie, founder of the Sisters of Notre Dame de Namur*

> *The heart that breaks open can contain the whole universe.*
> Joanna Macy

And then there is another Dorothy — Dorothy Mae Stang, a missionary sister of Notre Dame de Namur. She came from Dayton, Ohio, but became a Brazilian citizen who worked for more than forty years in the Anapu region of the Amazon with the poorest of the poor, the landless, the abandoned and the homeless. She was also a dedicated organizer and worked with many communities teaching sustainable farming, founding small base Christian communities that studied the Scriptures for conversion and doing justice work among groups living in the forests. She worked with the government — begging and pleading and protesting to get deeds for the people's land, and working with them for protection against violent attacks, constant harassment, and the physical and legal battles with the ranchers and loggers who plagued the people. She wanted for them what they wanted for themselves: safe drinking water, healthy food, a home that sheltered them from the elements, education, basic health care, and a piece of land that they could share with others, a place where they could make a living and live without fear with their children.

As often happens, for others her story begins outside her home in Brazil and her religious community — it begins with her death. Stang was in a remote settlement, Boa Esperança, in the Amazon forest, where she had been attending a meeting of poor farmers. The night before she was killed, the tension was high — between the farmers and the developers and wealthy ranchers who wanted the farmers' land. Ivan, the farmer who drove her out to the settlement, remembers that she said, "If anything happens, I hope it happens to me. The others have their families."[9]

Stang was seventy-three years old at the time, and she had long ago decided that her home was with the farmers and their families moving ever deeper into the forests, and that her place was with them as they struggled for justice for themselves, for the land, and for the forest. She was committed to the Project for Sustainable Development, which involved assisting rural farmers whom the government had awarded two huge parcels of land. She helped them in their efforts to stop the logging and ranching, and to reforest the area and practice sustainable farming. She had gotten used to receiving death threats from gunmen (hired by ranchers) who would illegally invade the area. She had testified in the State Senate, asking, "Have you ever heard a monkey sobbing in pain as his trees are being burned?" There were many who did not share either her concern for the reforestation or her solidarity with the farmers.

But she had her supporters too. She had written a letter to a donor expressing great hope:

> But if we keep working, helping our people grow in education, their ability to speak up — organize — create within themselves a *spirit* guided by *The Spirit* to help create a *new people* a little at a time, we'll get there. I might not live to see this day, but with the help of all of you, our people have grown in their understanding — caring for others.[10]

Stang had been at the work for a long time. By 2002, when she turned seventy, the work was becoming more physically demanding for her. She wrote to a friend, "Some of us are getting older, and our presence in the woods is lessening due to physical demands of walking long distances in the forest where there are no types of roads — just jungle paths." She knew that her strength had ebbed with the years. Still, she said,

> helping our people fight against logging firms and ruthless ranchers absorbs most of my time. I am here twenty years in this area [of] Anapu. I know well who has land *documentos* and the false maneuvering done by government agencies. In our home we receive groups of men running to us from the woods. They have been threatened, and their small families are asking for our support in facing the judicial processes thrown at them. We have at present some 500 to 600 families that have migrated this year to Anapu from areas that have been depleted, areas where there is drought. Our road was improved, and this is bringing these families.[11]

Biographer Roseanne Murphy describes the importance of Stang's works:

> Dorothy was the poor people's legal recourse. She was the one who knew the laws, the lawyers, and the government agencies to contact. The poor looked to her as their protector. But the government in the area had almost no power over the landowners, who paid

off anyone who might get in their way and who hired gunmen to "clear the area." Stang knew that the odds against getting any kind of just settlement in a land dispute were against the poor, but she never stopped trying.[12]

Because of her words and her work, there was a price on Stang's head. Whoever killed her would be paid 50,000 reais (about $20,000). But she was adamant about staying, Murphy points out:

"I know that they want to kill me, but I will not go away. My place is here alongside these people who are constantly humiliated by others who consider themselves powerful." She shared with a friend, "I have learned that faith sustains you, and I have also learned that three things are difficult: as a woman, to be taken seriously in the struggle for land reform; to stay faithful to believing that these small groups of poor farmers will prevail in organizing and carrying their own agenda forward; and to have the courage to give your life in the struggle to change." However, she thought that being an American and being "an old woman" would protect her. She was wrong.[13]

The night before Stang was actually killed, a landowner had hired two gunmen to do the job. The next morning — it was February 12, 2005 — Stang was walking up a hill in a soft rain. She was intent on getting to the meetingplace before everyone else arrived. The two men waited and watched for her.[14]

Stang had always loved the trees, and at the top of the hill she found herself standing under a canopy of towering ones. That's when the two men, whom she knew — Raifran and Clodoaldo — stepped out in front of her and blocked the way. She had a conversation with them on "the rights of the earth," on what not to plant that would destroy the environment, and she told them that she understood their position that they were like soldiers following orders. Her friend Cicero, who had been trying to catch up with her, saw her blocked by the two men and hid to see what would happen. At one point Stang was on her knees with a map, showing the two men that the land in question was in the reserves and could not be used for clear-cutting, development, or cattle ranching. Raifran stood by her, watching Clodoaldo (seated on a stump) for the signal to shoot her. Murphy describes what happened next:

> Dorothy stood up again. Raifran asked her if she had a weapon. She answered that the only weapon she had was her Bible, which she immediately produced from her bag. She read a passage about how God left all things for everyone to use, and then she read from the Beatitudes: "Blessed are the poor in spirit, for theirs is the kingdom of heaven; blessed are those who hunger and thirst for justice, for they shall be filled; blessed are the peacemakers, for they shall be called the children of God." (142)

When Stang finished reading, the two men again looked at each other but didn't fire. Stang invited them to come to the meeting, ending with "God bless you, my sons"; then she turned to walk up the hill. The men looked at each other again, and this time, Raifran got the signal. Clodoaldo called out after Stang, and when she turned, she saw Raifran standing by her, holding the gun. He said, "If you haven't solved this problem till now, you're not going to be around to solve it any longer" (142). She still held the Bible in her hand, and she raised it as if to protect herself. Then Raifran fired. The first bullet went through her hand into her abdomen, and she fell face down on the ground. Clodoaldo hid in the bushes, and Raifran moved in closer and fired again, hitting her in her shoulder from the back. Then he moved to her head and emptied his gun into her, taking four more shots. And then he ran.

As Stang lay bleeding on the ground, the rain continued. By the time Cicero and some of the farmers knew what had happened, she was dead. Her body lay on the ground all day, with the rain still coming down. The farmers grieved. But others rejoiced, shooting guns into the air and shouting, "Ah, you lost your madre! Who's going to protect you now?"

Eventually Stang was buried in Altamira. Sister Jo Anne officiated at the funeral. After she welcomed the many people who had gathered, she recalled a farmer's comment from the previous night. "Today," she said, "we are not going to *bury* Dorothy. We are to *plant* her." Then, raising her hands in the air, she exclaimed, "Dorothy vive!" and the shout came back again and again (151).

The sisters of Stang's community use her story as the inspiration for their mission — to become "Women with Hearts as Wide as the World." They want the story of the poor farmers in the Amazon to be remembered, and they want to raise awareness of the continuing environmental dangers caused by the ravaging of the Amazon.

On the first anniversary of Stang's death — February 12, 2006 — 820 white crosses were pounded into the ground near her grave. "Each cross represented either someone who had been murdered for working for justice or a poor farmer who had been killed in the Amazon during the last twenty years. In addition, there were seventy-two red crosses, representing those who had recently received death threats" (155). Antonia, one of the women leaders, drew all the women together, and they circled Stang's grave. Antonia to Dorothy on behalf of the people gathered there: "Dorothy, we promise to continue using your smile and your faith every day in our struggle, and to continue planting the seeds of love, peace, and social justice." And the response came back: "Dorothy vive!" Dorothy lives! (155). The people have named the place where she was martyred Hope, and they call her the eco-martyr of the Amazon.

Dorothy Day once said, "The only way to live in any true security is to live so close to the bottom that when you fall, you do not have much to lose or far to drop." Both she and Dorothy Stang lived by this principle. These two women honored the land and the sustenance it provided, and they honored other human beings — especially those neglected and hungry — and saw the intimate connection and power that braids the three together. Each woman suffered for crying out on behalf of others. But each still chose to take her few loaves and fishes and turn them into the miracle of feeding the people, setting them free, and giving them the hospitality of the land.

Sources Used in This Chapter

Sources on Dorothy Day

Jim Forest, "Dorothy Day: A Radical Simplicity," in *Cloud of Witnesses,* ed. Jim Wallis and Joyce Hollyday, rev. ed. Maryknoll, N.Y.: Orbis Books, 2005.

Don't Call Me a Saint. This film, produced by Claudia Larson, can be ordered from dorothydaydoc.com.

Dorothy Day: Selected Writings. Edited and with an introduction by Robert Ellsberg. Maryknoll, N.Y.: Orbis Books, 2009.

The Duty of Delight: The Diaries of Dorothy Day. Edited by Robert Ellsberg. Milwaukee: Marquette University Press, 2009.

Dan McKanan. *The Catholic Worker after Dorothy: Practicing the Works of Mercy in a New Generation.* Collegeville, Minn.: Liturgical Press, 2008.

Modern Spiritual Masters: Writings on Contemplation and Compassion. Edited by Robert Ellsberg. Maryknoll, N.Y.: Orbis Books, 2008. See "Dorothy Day: A New Kind of Holiness," pp. 161-81.

Susan Rakoczy. *Great Mystics and Social Justice: Walking on the Two Feet of Love.* Mahwah, N.J.: Paulist Press, 2006. See "Dorothy Day: Prophet of Poverty," pp. 135-59.

Sources on Dorothy Mae Stang

Binka Le Breton. *The Greatest Gift: The Courageous Life and Martyrdom of Sister Dorothy Stang.* New York: Doubleday, 2008.

"The Legacy of an Eco-martyr." Story and photos by Paul Jeffrey. *National Catholic Reporter,* 11 July 2008, pp. 11-13.

Roseanne Murphy. *Martyr of the Amazon: The Life of Sister Dorothy Stang.* Maryknoll, N.Y.: Orbis Books, 2007.

They Killed Sister Dorothy. This feature-length documentary, narrated by Martin Sheen and produced by Daniel Junge, is available at www.theykilledsisterdorothy.com.

Chapter 6

Raising Children from the Dead

Hope . . .
is the singular gift we cannot destroy in ourselves,
the argument that refutes death, the genius that invents
the future,
all we know of God.

Lisel Mueller, "Hope"

Among the Southwestern native peoples there is a strong symbol, a clay doll called the Storyteller. It is usually a woman seated on the ground, Mother the Earth, with her head tilted back toward the heavens, Father the Sky, with her mouth open — to draw in the breath of the Great Spirit and to sing and cry forth the stories of the people. She is rarely a singular figure — most often there are any number of children crawling up her torso, sitting in her lap, hanging onto her shoulders, piggy-back style, clinging with their arms around her neck, and sitting beside her. Traditionally the number of children — or animals and birds — that are around her are the number of stories that the teller is known for in her community, among her tribe. There are small dolls with one or two, maybe three children; there are larger dolls with a half dozen to a dozen or more; and there are huge dolls — life-sized ones — with hundreds and hundreds of tiny children and figures crawling up and down, living on the dolls' sturdy bodies. In Africa the person who is the storyteller is called a *griot* — the one who carries the stories of the people. The storyteller carries individuals' names and tribal connections, their lineages and their ancestors, those far back with roots in the past and roots in the sky where their spirits still look over those on earth. It is a burden to bear these lengthy tales and genealogies of all the members of the tribes, but it is also a high honor as well. For the people know that this person is entrusted with their names, their memories, their power, and the sources of their very bodies, families, and place in the world, past, present, and future — in their children and children's children. In a sense, these women and men carry the whole people and raise the children for succeeding generations.

In the West we often think of a family as mother, father, and child or children — the nuclear family. This is a very recent development — even the description of "nuclear" attests to its contemporary naming. Why anyone would name something that has to do with human beings "nuclear" is also indicative of what the family has come to mean in society. By its very nature, anything nuclear builds pressure and power within, self-contained, until it bursts asunder and explodes from the inside out — sadly, an apt description of family in many European and American cultures. We are even encouraged to model the Holy Family of Jesus, Mary, and Joseph — which ignores the obvious reality of Jesus' brothers and sisters: James, Joses, Judas, Simon, and Jesus' sisters (Mark 6:3). At the time of Jesus (and still today in most "underdeveloped countries") extended families related by blood and marriage clustered together in small villages, everyone being related to everyone else and everyone knowing the connections. It was and is a much tighter and a much looser society than what has "developed" in other parts of the world. In addition to these close "relatives," there were other tribes, those that traditionally would be eligible for marrying into and with, and those historically considered taboo because of past conflicts, present hostilities, and cultural differences. It was a world of ethnic minorities and majorities, tribalism, and nationalism based on these differences as well as religion, race, and gender.

At the time of Jesus, the Jewish people lived under Roman domination, and had lived that way for almost one hundred years, forcing the community closer together and making it more tightly controlled by the religious leadership. Survival meant that the Jewish people had to live as slaves on what was their own land, historically and religiously, and live within the shadow of violence and death; and that they had to live within their own community under tight laws and restrictions that were culturally and religiously enforced, which also had consequences for life and death. There is a story that is told only in the Gospel of Luke: the raising of the widow of Nain's son from the dead (Luke 7:11-17). Jesus has preached what is known as the Sermon on the Plain, with blessings and woes describing groups of people and their words and behaviors. He has talked about the importance of loving one's enemies and responding with dignity to beggars and outsiders, even those outside the law. He has called on the people to stop judging others and to look to the fruits of their own actions, and to lay a foundation based on both listening to his word and acting upon it. And in Luke's Gospel we read that Jesus has met with resistance, hatred, and angry threats to kill him from the very first time he preached in his own hometown synagogue of Nazareth (Luke 4). This is the setting for the story of the widow and her son.

> Soon afterward he journeyed to a city called Nain, and his disciples and a large crowd accompanied him. As he drew near to the gate of the city, a man who had died was being carried out, the only son of his mother, and she was a widow. A large crowd from the city was with her. When the Lord saw her, he was moved with pity for her and said to her, "Do not weep." (Luke 7:11-13)

The set-up of the story poses a number of issues that it helps to be aware of — part of the culture of Jewish familial and societal values and practices. The burial grounds or cemeteries were outside the boundaries of the town, and people lived in them — those cast off from the community because of sin, sickness, deformed bodies, and insanity; those associated with death; and those without any ties to family to provide for them. People are carrying out the widow's grown son to bury him there, and then they will leave her out there to die — or to survive as best she can on her own. It is her only son — who under the law would have been required to care for her until he was thirty years old or to take her in once he was married, so that she could live with his family. This was the law when a woman's husband had no brother to take her in, marry her, and raise up children with her — for her husband's name. So the death of this woman's son is her own death sentence in the community. She is not only grieving; she is bereft, lost, and about to be abandoned by all.

Jesus sees and hears about her situation and "is moved with pity for her." What we might find odd is what he says to her: "Do not weep." (Most likely he precedes his comment with "Woman," the formal title of honor.) If she is not to weep, then what is she to do? When this story is told aloud in a group, many women respond by saying that when someone tells them to stop crying, they cry and wail all the louder in protest and despair. They think they are not being heard or taken seriously. But oftentimes we weep instead of doing other things — like becoming angry, or confronting others, or facing a situation courageously and publicly. There is a saying in many African and indigenous cultures: "There is a time to stand up and show your soul — know when to let its light burst forth for all to see." Perhaps this is one of those times for this widow, now childless, orphaned, as well.

> He stepped forward and touched the coffin; at this the bearers halted, and he said, "Young man, I tell you, arise!" The dead man sat up and began to speak, and Jesus gave him to his mother. Fear seized them all, and they glorified God, exclaiming, "A great prophet has arisen in our midst," and "God has visited his people." This report about him spread through the whole of Judea and in all the surrounding region. (Luke 7:14-17)

What Jesus does is shocking! He touches the bier that bears the dead and thus unclean body of the young man. Jesus himself is now unclean. He has put himself solidly with the widow and the dead man, aligned himself with them — as though he is saying, "Bury him, abandon her — then you abandon me and bury me too." They are supposedly grieving with her, and perhaps some do actually care for her, but because of the law and custom, there is no one who will take her in and act upon their feelings or their voiced concerns. There is a mixture of anger and compassion in Jesus' pity. In fact, the word for *pity* in Greek is almost visceral — indicating the sight of something that makes you so sick you want to vomit and/or the sight of something that makes you so angry that you go into labor pains to give birth to something new to alter the existing reality. It is a powerful word often used to describe Jesus' feelings and what drives him to act on behalf of others — sometimes even whole crowds of people in desperate need or a desperate situation.

Then Jesus' words shock! "Young man, I tell you, arise!" Get up and walk away from being dead! And in that moment, Jesus raised two people from the dead — the young man and the widow who was being condemned to death because of his death. And the dead man hears Jesus' voice and obeys his word — and he sits up and begins to talk! One wonders what he said! And then Jesus gives him to his mother — an echo of the prophet Elijah, who gave back to the widow of Zarephath her child, who died but came to life again because Elijah had prayed to God for his life (1 Kings 17:17-24). It is the tradition in Israel that a man or woman of God has the power of the word of God in his or her mouth, and that word can bring life back to the dead.

And the people respond accordingly — "This person is of God! A great prophet has arisen in our midst! God has visited his people!" This visitation of God among the people was the presence of a prophet, an angel, a message from God. It was to be heeded, and transformation was to follow. Jesus' intervention on behalf of the widow is a condemnation of the people's custom — to leave another to die, to abandon those without family, those utterly alone and destitute because of a lack of ties to blood relatives. The custom must be abandoned. The community must take in all those who find themselves in such a situation, and it must give life back to them, adopting them as parents and elders among them, with honor. No one is to be abandoned or orphaned or condemned to a life sentence that can only end in a slow, painful, lonely death.

This is the biblical story that I have chosen to tell to frame the story of a most remarkable woman who found herself in a brutal, violent, and inhuman situation. It is the only story that comes close to speaking about the experience of this contemporary woman. Her story has

100

one major difference that compounds the problems and the horror. It is the reverse of the story of the widow of Nain: the parents are tortured and beheaded in front of their children, and the children are left with the memory and the traumas — often tortured and maimed themselves, and abandoned in huge numbers to fend for themselves in a country that is devastated — torched and looted. It is the story of genocide in so many countries, but specifically in Burundi in 1993, when there were massacres between two tribes: the Hutus and the Tutsis. The Hutus were 98 percent of the population ruled by the minority tribe of Tutsis, known for their ferocious treatment of those they ruled over.

The woman whose story I want to tell is Marguerite Barankitse, a Tutsi, born in the mid-1940s, called Maggy by everyone. In the Kirundi language of her native Burundi, her original surname, Habonimana, means "God is watching." But her father died when she was five, and her mother changed their name to Barankitse, meaning "God has a grudge against me." Both her names speak volumes about her life and what she has become. Marguerite means "pearl of great price." This name too fits her gracefully and truthfully. It recalls the parable of the pearl, a symbol of the kingdom of abiding justice and peace that is worth so much more than all else that we should spend our time — our whole lives — seeking it and rejoice exceedingly upon finding it.

Barankitse was born in the third-poorest country in the world and brought up in Ruyigi, close to the border of Tanzania, a place with a long history of ethnic discrimination that erupted in 1993 in a bloodbath of hatred and revenge. Barankitse went to Catholic schools, but she often says that it was her mother who educated her:

Mother never locked the front door. She said we were all God's children. On Sundays we would visit neighbors or the sick, taking them banana wine or sorgo beer. When the children demanded meat at meals, she would laugh and say, "There's more protein in beans." Her mother died in 1989, leaving her daughter with a heart of gold and lively sense of humor.[1]

Barankitse followed early in the footsteps of her mother. Before she ever married, she adopted her first child, Chloe, a thirteen-year-old girl, in 1976. Chloe's father was killed in 1972, when 150,000 Hutus were slaughtered by the Tutsi authorities. Her mother died a few years later, and Barankitse took her in. She said in an interview, "I took Chloe to show it could be different — her father was killed by Tutsis, and I would raise her. There was room in my house, and that's what my mother taught me." Soon after, Barankitse was engaged to be married, but her fiance's relatives were horrified that a Hutu child would be joining the family when the marriage took place. She told them, "It's both of us or neither." And she has never married. And in the intervening years she adopted six more foster children — seven in all: three Tutsis and four Hutus.

She became a teacher and an administrator. She was working at the bishop's palace in Ruyigi when the killing began in 1993. It was triggered by the assassination of Burundi's first democratically elected president, a Hutu. The Hutus blamed the Tutsi elite, and they attacked, and then the Tutsi army retaliated in kind, driving terrified people down from the hills. Barankitse brought them inside the palace compound and sheltered as many as she could. She and her children and seventy-three Hutus took shelter in the church. It was the Tutsis, some of them Barankitse's own relatives, who broke in. It was October 24. They chained her to a chair, stripped her, and forced her to watch while they butchered seventy-three people, men and women, young and old, in front of her, dismembering them and burning them alive, all the while beating her relentlessly. One of the women, who was a dear friend of hers, cried out her last words to her: "You must raise our children."

Later, in interviews, Barankitse would explain why she does what she does. The sight of a few children who had been spared sparked her determination to stay alive, a determination that she has never lost since. Her fate was settled. "I said no, once and for all, to such hatred," she explained. "With the education I had received, there was no way I could allow the very best in life to be destroyed." That day in the church, twenty-five children were orphaned. Barankitse took the little money she had access to and ransomed them all from the killing mob. Then she found an abandoned house — as she says, to "cache them in" — and over the next weeks she foraged and stole, borrowed and begged to feed them and take care of them. In the beginning, she said, it was the rage that kept her alive. They had nothing. They were constantly improvising, sharing, making cots out of cardboard. They threw nothing away. They did anything and everything just to stay alive.[2]

This abandoned house became her first Maison Shalom in Ruyigi, in 1994, sixteen years ago, when she was thirty-eight. And the children just kept coming. Within months there were sixty-five children; within a year, there were 160. Now she's fifty-five, and there are ten thousand children — all "Maggie's children" — in Maison Shalom shelters spread all across Burundi. She says with her cascading, rippling laugh "that she's been much too busy raising children to think about, well, having children."[3]

Now the shelters include a garage where former child soldiers repair vehicles and learn trades under the watchful, caring eyes of those who function as aunts and uncles and grandparents. There is also a hair salon, a cinema (the only one in the country in 2006), a pair of guesthouses, a public swimming pool, a library, and five "villages" and farms where paid caregivers raise orphans in small family homes and provide food for all as well as supplying other houses. Barankitse engages elders from the village to live with the children, and she seeks to teach them all how to farm — which is how 90 percent of Burundians survive.

In the beginning, all the children were orphans of the massacres, suffering from rape, abuse, maiming, disease, starvation — all of them traumatized by what they had seen and endured, some mute and catatonic. All of their parents had been killed in the war. Finally there was a cease-fire in 2003, and Barankitse began the rigorous and detailed work of tracing surviving family members to the refugee camps and seeking relatives in the children's original villages. Now over five thousand of the children have gone back to family homes.

Today, Maison Shalom still takes in orphans, but it also takes in other victims — persons struggling with HIV/AIDS and hunger. Most are children, but Barankitse takes in adults too: mothers with far-advanced AIDS who give birth to their children before they die (this is the fastest-growing group since the cease-fire); people just out of prison, prostitutes, and victims of rape with nowhere to go; and scores of refugees from the camps in nearby Tanzania and Rwanda.

It hasn't been easy. Barankitse is Tutsi, and her own people branded her a traitor; the Hutus persecuted her as a spy. She says no one trusted her, and there was constant verbal abuse and property damage and theft — her car torched, her houses broken into, her cows stolen. Yet when she was interviewed by police, she repeated what her mother had told her: "We do not lock our doors. If people need to steal a cow, they must be hungry. I can always replace cows." But she is fierce in her protection of her children. She knows each by name, and she knows each of their stories. And they call her their Angel of Burundi; they are her children. They wait for her presence among them, cling to her long skirts and burrow between her knees and into her arms. She bends over them and hugs them, holds them and laughs with them, touching them all with love and sheer delight. In an interview with Stephanie Nolen in Ruyigi, she walks around explaining who is who. "That one," she begins, "I found, still tied to her mother's back, in a pile of corpses. A grenade had blown off most of his face. This one, his mother died of AIDS. Now that one, she's a child of rape — her mother was raped by the rebels. And that one too." Nolen continues,

> Marguerite Barankitse makes her way through a crowd of children in this town in the Burundi highlands. She stops here and there to wipe a crusty nose, shoo away the flies, and scoop a fat toddler up for a cuddle, talking all the while. These are Maggy's children: there are 10,000 of them, and she knows each one.[4]

After sixteen years, Barankitse's work has drawn international recognition and honors. She is shrewd and wise as well as loving and tender. She can be tough as nails, speaking words that can have the force of blunt hammerblows. Her children, growing up now, many in their twenties and thirties, are inspired by her, utterly grateful to her, in awe of her, and want to be just like her. Some say the number of children she has raised is closer to fifty thousand and still rising. She has won the Nansen Prize from the United Nations High Commissioner for Refugees (2005). Her work is spreading into Rwanda and the Congo, but she has bigger dreams. In the interview with Nolen, she's forceful and to the point:

I'm told when I beg there isn't enough money. But now I've been outside Africa — to Rome, to New York and Paris — and I look around — "No money!?!" What do you waste in arms and weapons? If you — the United States, any country — would give me just a quarter of it, every child in the world could have immunization, health care, education. Keep your other three-quarters, but give me one-quarter. And we'll make a revolution of love![5]

Barankitse is equally demanding and truthful when dealing with the Catholic Church in her country. She's a frequent visitor to the Vatican, recently attending the African Synod of Bishops (October 2008) as a participant. Along with other women, she demanded that the church do more than talk about the dignity of women. They tried to make the bishops of the universal church imagine what the church without women would be like — unthinkable! Well, if that was true, then open up positions of responsibility to them, in parishes and dioceses as theologians, preachers, and teachers, and in places where the decisions are being made — make women equal partners with you.

In Africa, 75 percent of the church's populations are women (and not just the Catholic church but the evangelical and Pentecostal ones as well). And yet, Barankitse is quick to point out that women are marginalized at every point in life and society, and they are the first to suffer in genocide and war, as well as in hard economic times. It is the women who do the work of forgiveness, reconciliation, and rebuilding of the communities among those who did the killings and those who were the victims and survivors — many of these women are called the Ladies of Divine Mercy. And they're the ones who teach alternatives to retaliation and vengeance and who seek to lift the burden of hate, distrust, and despair from the hearts of all the people. They are the ones who are actually convening what would be called local truth commissions in all the villages and leading the people in rituals of healing and forgiveness between bitter enemies and giving them the resources to live in peace together. They do not forget; they create something other, something graced and new, born of pity, wisdom, and hope, reestablishing mutual liberation and a possibility of living together in harmony once again.

Barankitse was one of three African women who gave testimony at the Rimini meeting in Rome. She told the bishops that many call her a madwoman back home, and that she has long challenged the church, her country, and her own communities with the reality of what they have done themselves, and what the terrible consequences have been and still are. They are one of the poorest countries on earth. Their life expectancy is thirty-nine for women and forty-two for men, and one in every five of its 6.8 million people is infected with AIDS. And poverty hits the women hardest, through ignorance about contraception and lack of education.

Barankitse has said in interviews that "I have two very sick relatives, Burundi and the church." And she has short shrift with most of the clergy: "I cannot stand them anymore. They preach, quote dogma, and excommunicate sinners: 'Thou shalt not do this, or that.' But they completely forget the message of Christ, who forgave sinners like Mary Magdalene and loved them." And she herself knows much about forgiveness. She speaks of many of the people she still has to go to church with, people who once said they were her friends — people she saw torturing and killing without shame — "murdering their own brothers and sisters — I had to make a huge effort to keep saying to myself: 'Maggy, Jesus loves them too, even if they are criminals.'"[6]

There is a parable — some say it is a Buddhist koan, others say it is a story from Africa — based in part on what is sometimes called the poisonwood tree (a tree made famous by Barbara Kingsolver in her novel *The Poisonwood Bible*. In the novel, a southern Baptist missionary preacher, Reverend Nathan Price, harangues his Congolese villagers. He is constantly trying to say that Jesus is supreme, but instead, because he doesn't listen and doesn't understand the villagers' language, he keeps preaching that Jesus is poisonwood — a local plant that gives those who come in contact with it horribly irritating and painful stings and rashes. The preacher sticks rigidly to his King James Version of the Bible, unaware of what he's preaching and screaming out so aggressively every Sunday morning — never thinking that people are not coming because of him, his attitude, and the words coming out of his mouth.[7]

The story I mentioned earlier is called "The Poison Tree." This is the way I tell it.

Once upon a time, there was a village on the edge of the forest. One afternoon, one of the villagers happened to be walking near the edge of the village and noticed a tree he did not remember being there before. He approached it, and as he investigated it, he realized to his horror that it was a dreaded poison tree. Where did it come from? Did someone plant it? Did a bird carry the seed, or was it dropped in dung? How long had the tree been growing there, with no one noticing what it was or the terrible danger it presented just by being on the edge of the village? It was a threat to everyone who lived there and everyone who walked by on the road. Immediately the man ran into the village, crying out and gathering everyone in its center, telling them what he had found.

The people were equally upset and concerned, even terrified. They had heard stories since they were young. They had been told what the tree was like and that its poison was vicious. Most people who came into contact with it died slow, horrible deaths, and those who survived did not consider themselves fortunate, because they were scarred and often plagued by returning fevers and chills and a terrible sickness. The villagers screamed back and forth at each other — all intent on doing something to get rid of the tree as soon as possible. Some said, "We must get rid of it tomorrow — it must be chopped down!"

"No," others said, "that's too dangerous — just touching it or the sap can infect you. It has to be burned down and the roots dug out and burned too." The tree was to be treated as a dangerous enemy to all. But some of the elders tried a bit of restraint. "No, we don't have to destroy it. We just don't know a lot about it, except hearsay and the fears it causes. We need to find out more about it — where it comes from and what it can do for good as well as evil. We can build a fence around it and put up a sign that says, 'Unknown Danger — Keep Out.' After all, the Creator made it along with all the other trees — it has to have some good in it."

The villagers argued most of the night. Finally they decided to go to bed and deal with the tree in the morning.

The very next morning as the people were gathering again, a stranger came into town, excited and breathless from running — she said she had been running for many days. She had heard from other villagers who had taken the road close to this village that they had a poison tree — not a small seedling, but an actual tree with branches, leaves, and buds of some sort that would flower. And the tree was healthy — they could tell it had strong roots because of its sap and girth. The villagers were silent.

The stranger continued, "I am a healer, and we are in desperate need of the tree's remedies. We make tinctures, teas, salves from it. Even its moss heals and eases throats, lungs, skin, headaches, anxiety, kidney and liver ailments, and strengthens the heart. We keep learning more and more of what it can do. It's true that it can wound you, scratch you, and give you a terrible rash, but if you learn how to ingest it and make it part of your own body, it has amazing healing capacities. Some of our most potent medicines come from this tree, and so many of them have been destroyed, burned, and cut down, chopped to pieces, that it's hard to find one. Please tell me where it is so that I might go and honor it, and then take some of its leaves, bark, buds, sap, and even a few pieces of its roots so that I may take them home with me and transplant them — perhaps one or two of the root pieces you let me have will take root near our village. Please," she said, "would you be willing to share some of your tree as a gift between our villages?"

The villagers were stunned. [And there is a saying among tellers: "And the story begins when the teller stops talking."]

This is a most wondrous story about what poison is — hatred, war, brutality, killing, murder, torture, blood feuds, vengeance, the refusal to forgive — and what it can be transformed into by love, hope, mercy, and stubborn life.

Marguerite Barankitse has learned indeed that "God is watching" and that "God has a grudge against me" — she knows that our lives can carry great violence as well as great love at their roots. And Barankitse has found the "pearl of great price" — a revolution of love. Raising children takes a power and a gift at least as important as that of giving birth to children. The way we treat other people's children — not our own — is the indicator of our love and justice, our service and worship of God. The Angel of Burundi is a tall, regal woman of flesh and blood and a great wide heart that can know and love tens of thousands of children, no matter what race or tribe or country they come from — they are all brothers and sisters, they are all God's children — and they are all her children.

In a recent interview at the African Synod in Rome, Barankitse said that she sees all things in her life as "the fruits of love" — not only whatever prizes she receives, and the children who see themselves as her children, but also the beatings and betrayals she has experienced.

She affirmed that at first, she wondered why the God of love would allow such things. "I saw in the eyes of children a hope that was not extinguished and began to understand that God was answering me through their gaze."[8]

Sources Used in This Chapter

"Burundi 'Angel' Tells of Rescuing Children: African Testimonies Impact Rimini Meeting." *Zenit,* 28 August 2008. See http://www.zenit.org/article-23494?1=english.

Anthony Faiola. "Women Take Charge in Rwanda." *Washington Post* article appearing in *Guardian Weekly,* Manchester, England, 13 June 2008, p. 42.

Peter Feuerherd. "Immaculee Ilibagiza: Forgiveness amidst Despair." *St. Anthony Messenger,* pp. 28-32.

Soren Gordhamer. "Bringing Mindfulness Practices to Rwanda." *Inquiring Mind,* Spring 2009, p. 28.

Immaculee Ilibagiza with Steve Erwin. *Left to Tell: Discovering God amidst the Rwandan Holocaust.* Carlsbad, Calif.: Hay House, 2006. See also www.lefttotell.com and a documentary film titled *The Diary of Immaculee.*

"Marguerite Barankitse, Africa's Answer to Mother Teresa, Talks to Henri Tincq about Her Life's Work." *Guardian Weekly,* Manchester, England, April 28-May 4, 2006.

Suzanne St. Yves. "Peace Activist 'Just an Ordinary Village Woman.'" *Prairie Messenger,* Saskatoon, Saskatchewan, Canada, 30 April 2008.

Alice Walker. "Overcoming Speechlessness: A Poet Encounters 'the Horror' in Rwanda, Eastern Congo, and Palestine/Israel." *Tikkun* magazine, September/October 2009, pp. 33-38, 86-89.

Cindy Wooden. "Women at Synod Urge Bishops to Foster Equality." *Prairie Messenger,* Saskatoon, Saskatchewan, Canada, 14 October 2009, p. 16.

Chapter 7

Midwives of Peace

Reverence declares: "All the things God established please me. I do not hurt any of them."

Hildegard of Bingen

How does one begin to speak of violence, murder, legalized killing, torture, rape, the destruction of the earth and its inhabitants — the stupid and irrational decision to attack others, to maim, inflict pain, commit horror, and then to glorify it, praise it, and refer to those who do such things as heroes and heroines — what is called war, but in reality is purely and simply evil — always a disaster for humankind. All of the evils described and resisted in this chapter are the opposite of anything that is religious or spiritual, worthy of worship, or the essence and heart of what it means to be human beings made in the image and likeness of God.

During World War II, a young woman, Etty Hillesum, was last seen dropping postcards out of a boxcar on October 10, 1943. She — along with her mother, father, brother Mischa, and 987 other people (among them 170 children) — were on their way to the concentration camp at Westerbork. Only eight people survived the horrors there.

Just days before she died in the camp, Hillesum wrote these words in her journal:

There is no hidden poet in me, just a little piece of God that might grow into poetry. And a camp needs a poet, one who experiences life there, even there, as a bard and is able to sing about it.

At night, as I lay in the camp on my plank bed, surrounded by women and girls gently snoring, dreaming aloud, quietly sobbing, and tossing and turning, women and girls who often told me during the day, "We don't want to think, we don't want to feel — otherwise we are sure to go out of our minds." I was sometimes filled with an infinite tenderness, and lay awake for hours letting the gall of the many, too many impressions of a much-too-long day wash over me, and I prayed, "Let me be the thinking heart of these barracks." And that is what I want to be again. The thinking heart of a whole concentration camp.

October 3, 1942, Sunday morning[1]

This is the attitude and expression of a mature human being. It is someone capable of solidarity with others, of compassion, of love for all, even her enemies and those who persecute and harm her. It is someone capable of forgiveness and reverence, of being human in the face of inhumanity and despicable destruction of other human beings. These are also the characteristics of a mature believer in God, any God worth worshiping. It is far too easy to harm and kill; it is more indicative of strength, courage, and right to be able to love, love ever more abundantly all peoples, and to practice nonviolence, always seeking a creative and life-enhancing way to live in all situations.

In this chapter we will look at many women who have resisted and continue living lives of resistance, of mercy, and of compassion in the face of horror and what human beings (mostly men) have practiced as war in the last hundred years — the century that is already remembered for the slaughter of more human beings than have been violently killed in all of history's reckoning. These women all share the gift of giving birth to peace, the art of midwifery, the hard and sometimes bloody (from their own blood) resistance to the taking of life that is touted as patriotic, religious, necessary, bound to glory, and/or nationalistic, but is always just evil. Opposite to the act of war-making is the act of love-making.

111

In ancient Greece, Aristophanes wrote a play called *Lysistrata*. It tells the tale of what is probably the first strike by women against men to stop a war. It is the women of Athens, Sparta, Corinth, and Boeotia who resist: there will be no love-making, no sex, no intimacy between man and woman, no children born until the war is stopped once and for all. On stage, the strike ends in peace — but that was only on stage, not in reality. When the play was first performed, the war had been raging for twenty years, and it went on for seven more. Oddly enough, women were not allowed on stage and could not be actors, so there were no women in *Lysistrata* — all the roles were played by men in masks. But the idea was spoken out loud and acted in public, and now it is part of our culture and tradition. Perhaps it needs to be practiced in earnest more often these days.

We will begin by going back to the Franco-Prussian War and the woman who imagined the first Mother's Day: Julia Ward Howe. It was 1870, and she worked tirelessly for the nonviolent resolution of conflict and international solidarity between all women. The war had made her a pacifist, and her beliefs extended into her work to abolish slavery and to bring equality to women. She died in 1910, four years before President Wilson proclaimed the second Sunday in May as Mother's Day as "a public expression of our love and reverence for the mothers of our country." But that day has been shorn of all resemblance to what Julia Howe intended. Listen to just the first several lines from her call to arms!

> Arise then . . . women of this day!
> Arise, all women who have hearts!
> Whether your baptism be of water or of tears!
> Say firmly: "We will not have questions answered by irrelevant agencies. Our husbands will not come to us, reeking with carnage, for caresses and applause. Our sons will not be taken from us to unlearn all that we have been able to teach them of charity, mercy, and patience. We, the women of one country, will be too tender of those of another country to allow our sons to be trained to injure theirs."
> From the voice of a devastated Earth, a voice goes up with our

112

own. It says: "Disarm! Disarm! The sword of murder is not the balance of justice." Blood does not wipe away our dishonor, nor violence indicate possession. As men have often forsaken the plough and the anvil at the summons of war, let women now leave all that may be left of home for a great and earnest day of counsel.

Mother's Day is about arms — the kind referred to on a bumper sticker that says, "Arms are for hugging." The use of arms twisted into weapons of destruction is an untruth that must be resisted. "Disarm! Disarm!" Drop the weapons and the sick reasoning of making war and learn to look on others as human beings all sharing the same blood and the same desires for peace.

> *God has made of one blood all nations under heaven. No man can suddenly become my enemy just because he happened to have been born on the other side of a river or a boundary line, and his government has issued an ultimatum against mine. Is it not time that we refused to fight?*
> Muriel Lester, social reformer and pacifist, 1883-1968

But the Franco-Prussian War was followed by World War I, called the Great War, and a woman by the name of Kaethe Kollwitz, an artist and sculptor, was beginning to sense the madness that was growing all around her in Berlin. Then her son Peter was conscripted into the military. She wrote in her diary,

> Where do all these women find the courage to send their dear ones to the front to face the guns, when they have watched over them all their lives with such loving care? I fear that the despondency which is bound to follow will be all the blacker for the present mood of exaltation. . . .

She continued a month later,

> The idea of mere boys going into battle strikes me as senseless. It is all so pointless, so insane. . . . It's enough to drive one to despair.[2]

Her beloved Peter was killed two days after he reached the front lines. Within months, Kollwitz knew that she had to sculpt a memorial for him and for so many others who had died and were dying. She worked on different pieces, doing drawings for more than fifteen years. She was torn by grief and loss and the guilt that perhaps she was part of the war that had taken two million German soldiers. She was a pacifist — perhaps she should have tried harder to stop her son from joining up. It was not until 1931 that she finally finished a sculpture that she thought was fitting. It is two figures, her husband and herself: she is kneeling, bent over in mourning; her husband has his head thrown back in grief. Kollwitz told people that the figures were not just her and her husband but all the parents of their generation, weeping in grief, but also asking forgiveness of the next generation for having led them into war. Fittingly, the piece is called *Trauerndes Ehepaar,* meaning "Grieving Parents." Originally it was in a Flemish cemetery of Roggevelde, but it has been moved to the cemetery in Vladslo, Belgium, where the Kollwitzes' son was buried.

In 1933 Hitler rose to power, and Kollwitz and all her drawings, ink sketches, sculptures, and other pieces were declared "unpatriotic." She was harassed and considered "degenerate" along with her art. Everything was removed from galleries and public places, and she was stripped of her honors, including being the first woman of the Prussian Academy of the Arts. From then on she moved from place to place, a refugee. Her husband died, and her grandson, another soldier, was killed, and she could not stay in Berlin. She died on April 22, 1945, just days before Hitler's suicide. And yet, those who knew her said she still lived with hope, still continued to draw in ink and pencil, using mud — and, when she could, clay and stone — to sculpt pieces. One of her last entries in her journal echoes her hope:

> One day, a new ideal will arise, and there will be an end to all wars. I die convinced of this. It will need much hard work, but it will be achieved. . . . The important thing, until that happens, is to hold one's banner high and to struggle. . . . Without struggle there is no life.[3]

Kollwitz's writings and art are not only a testimony to peace and a protest against war. They are also a monument to birth, to life, and to peace with freedom. They reveal a depth of tenderness and earthiness that is both heart-breaking and life-giving.

> *When I dare to be powerful — to use my strength in the service of my vision — then it becomes less and less important whether I am afraid.*
>
> Audre Lorde

There is a story told in El Salvador over the last decades. Eduardo Galeano tells it in one of his latest books, *Voices of Time: A Life in Stories.*[4] It drives home what it is like to live in a climate of fear and terror, a region plagued by occupation, private and rebel armies, the shadow of war.

The Anatomy of Fear

The day is born, touched by the sun's fingers.

In the countryside of El Salvador, women light fires and begin their chores. "How did you dawn?" they ask, because, like the day, they dawn.

And by their bodies they know what the new day will bring. During the war years, every woman's body at dawn was a map of fear. If fear pressed against her breasts, one of her sons would not return. A sharp pain in the belly meant the army was approaching. And if her kidneys ached, there would not be enough water in the well and she would have to risk their lives searching for more.[5]

This is the reality of life for the majority of people in the world today. And it matters not what religious belief they practice — and what religion is practiced by those who attack. It is all sacrilege, desecration, and insult to God. For believers in God, perhaps one of the hardest things to do is to live with, forgive, and redeem what religious people do, often in the name of their God, to other people.

There is a terrible story in Matthew's Gospel that is part of the Christmas story — the birth of Jesus — that has much to say to Christians (and others) about violence, the killing of the innocent, nationalism, the orders to massacre, and power. It also has much to say about resistance, courage, flight, faithful endurance, and grief — and where God stands in the midst of such hatred, callousness, and killing.

The child Jesus has been born in Bethlehem of Judea, and magi — astrologers — come from the East (near Persia or perhaps even farther away). They stop at Herod's court to ask where the "new born king of the Jews can be found." Herod plays them, seeking information — asking his own astrologers and scribes where the child is. He tells the magi to return after they have found him, so that he too can go and pay homage to this child. The magi go, the star they followed returns to guide them, and they give the child their gifts. After being warned in a dream not to return to the palace, they return home by another route (Matt. 2:1-12).

When Herod realized that he had been deceived by the magi, he became furious. He ordered the massacre of all the boys in Bethlehem and its vicinity two years old and under, in accordance with the time he had ascertained from the magi. Then was fulfilled what had been said through Jeremiah the prophet:

"A voice was heard in Ramah, sobbing and loud lamentation; Rachel weeping for her children, and she would not be consoled, since they were no more." (Matt. 2:16-18, quoting Jer. 31:15)

Earlier in the story, when Herod hears about the possibility of a child being born that will usurp his throne and take his power, he becomes "greatly troubled, and all Jerusalem with him" (Matt. 2:3). The connection between the leader and the people of a kingdom or nation is intimate and has massive consequences. The power of a leader — based on personal feelings of inadequacy, fear, revenge, the need to assert power, even whim — is staggering. And his personal orders to the military that pledges allegiance to him (not the people) are fundamental to the exercise of violence. In this instance, Herod feels that he has been personally tricked — what he himself sought to do with the magi — and he acts in retaliation and rage, but also in self-interest. This is a man who is so insecure that the possibility of a child — one of his own people, even — one day taking his place as king, is enough to start a bloodbath that encompasses anyone who is guilty by association. Just being in the targeted geographical vicinity, the targeted age group, and the targeted gender group will be enough for scores of innocents to meet with the death sentence. We look at this as madness, but it is the way of war: the innocent are the first to suffer, and women and children are the victims to a far greater extent than any doing the fighting and the killing.

This is an important reality to look into — counting the number of victims. How many children died in Bethlehem and its vicinity? How many parents grieved? How many dreams were aborted? How many lives were disrupted and changed forever? In a war, how many rapes are committed? How many civilians are killed — on both sides? Those people and nations that have not experienced the ongoing brutality of war and its consequences in their lifetime — how do they begin to realize the breadth of killing and abuse? When questioned about how many Iraqi civilians had been killed by the American forces in March 2002, General Tommy Franks said, "We don't do body counts." Yet the United States had been claiming that it was going to great lengths to protect civilians. This statement contributed to an outburst of verbal rage in the Arab world because it suggested that the people of Iraq were bodies, not people. Since the war began almost a decade ago (this is the second Iraqi offensive — the first was in the early 1990s), the list of those in the military who have died is posted every day in every newspaper in Iraq. A meticulous count is kept.

Just recently, in November 2009, statistics were released about the number of innocents killed and injured:

For example, this month the Iraqi Human Rights Ministry released a report that shows 85,594 of its country's people were killed from 2004 to 2008 as a result of the U.S.-led invasion and 147,195 were wounded during the same period. Other estimates have arrived at much higher numbers.

All of the estimates, however, fail to take into account the women, children, and sometimes men whose lives are lost as a result of war-induced domestic and interpersonal violence. It can be difficult to obtain these numbers, but it must be tried. When something isn't counted, it often becomes invisible.[6]

There was a woman, Marla Ruzicka, who sought to count and publish the number of deaths in Iraq, often referred to as "damage assessment" or "collateral damage." She spent two years in Iraq, founding the Campaign for Innocent Victims in Conflict (www.civicworldwide .org) and organized groups across Iraq to document casualties. Before that, she had done similar work in Afghanistan, securing assistance for the survivors. And her life was summed up in a paragraph that appeared in *USA Today* on April 28, 2005:

> The writer, a 28-year-old humanitarian aid worker from California, was killed Saturday in Baghdad when a suicide bomber aiming for a convoy of contractors pulled alongside her vehicle and detonated his explosives. Her longtime driver and translator, Faiz Ali Salim, also died. She filed this piece from Baghdad a week before her death.
>
>> In my two years in Iraq, the one question I am asked the most is: "How many Iraqi civilians have been killed by American forces?" The American public has a right to know how many Iraqis have lost their lives since the start of the war and as hostilities continue.
>>
>> . . . Recently, I obtained statistics on civilian casualties from a high-ranking U.S. military official. The numbers were for Baghdad only, for a short period, during a relatively quiet time. Other hot spots, such as the Ramadi and Mosul area, proved worse. The statistics showed that 29 civilians were killed by small-arms during firefights between U.S. troops and insurgents between Feb. 28 and March 8 — four times the number of Iraqi police killed in the same period. It is not reported whether the bullets that killed these civilians were fired by U.S. troops or by insurgents.
>>
>> . . . A number is important not only to quantify the cost of war, but as a reminder of those whose dreams will never be realized in a free and democratic Iraq.[7]

Why is this important — this counting? Nicole Sotelo in her "Column/Opinion" in the *National Catholic Reporter* explains what follows after the conflicts cease or soldiers return home. What she reports is chilling:

> While violence against women has always been a part of war lore, it wasn't until the second half of the last century that people began collecting statistics on the topic. The studies reveal a gruesome pattern: Violence from the battlefield boils over into violence in the home due to post-traumatic stress disorder and the learned violence of war. If there was already violence in the home, it often escalates during internal or international conflict.
>
>   . . . A story done by the Iraq Psychologists Association found that of 2,500 families interviewed, 91 percent of children faced more aggression at home than they did before the U.S.-led invasion of 2003. . . . Of these, nearly 38 percent were reported to have had severe hematomas after beatings by their parents.
>
>   . . . The numbers are shocking in the United States also. Soldiers who come home from fighting abroad bring the war with them. Whether it is Vietnam, Iraq, or Afghanistan, the battlefields change from forests or deserts to United States bedrooms. The Miles Foundation reports that military families in the United States have a two to five times higher domestic violence rate than the general population.[8]

If the ratio of women and children to men in crowds is about five or six to one, as many sociologists calculate, then the number of rapes, beatings, killings, and other forms of abuse that the innocent face is far worse than anything being reported. In the Gospel account, all of this is intimated with one line: "A voice was heard in Ramah, sobbing and loud lamentation; Rachel weeping for her children, and she would not be consoled, since they were no more" (Matt. 2:18). A note in the New American Bible extends the meaning geographically and into other generations:

> Jeremiah 31:15 portrays Rachel, wife of the patriarch Jacob, weeping for her children taken into exile at the time of the Assyrian in-

vasion of the northern kingdom (722-21 BC). Bethlehem was traditionally identified with Ephrath, the place near which Rachel was buried (see Gen. 35:18; 48:7), and the mourning of Rachel is here applied to her lost children of a later age. Ramah is about six miles north of Jerusalem. The lamentation of Rachel is so great as to be heard at a far distance.

In the story, there is a paragraph found between the story of the magi honoring the child Jesus and the slaughter of the boy children his age and in his locale. In it, Joseph has a dream where he is told to escape, to get up immediately and run, taking the child and his mother and going into exile in Egypt. This period of exile was thought to be as long as six years or more. It seems that in times of war and violence, one must know when to run, when to hide, and where to hide. Egypt, once the place of bondage for Israelites, had become in the Old Testament a place of refuge for many being persecuted in Palestine.

Courage is the price that life exacts for granting peace.

Amelia Earhart

There are tales told about those who sheltered the child Jesus and his parents on the way to Egypt and how they lived there for years. When Herod was dead, they returned not to Bethlehem but to Nazareth, where no one would think to look for them. Who actually did help them out? Of course, there is no way of knowing.

But during World War II there was a Polish social worker in Warsaw's Department of Social Services, Irena Sendler, who was twenty-nine when the war broke out. The occupation of the Warsaw Ghetto began earlier, in 1939, but by 1942 it was clear to everyone what was intended: the enslavement, humiliation, and extermination of the Jews and other groups, because they lived in occupied territory. In Poland, to help a Jew was punishable by the death penalty.

Sendler belonged to a newly formed group, the Council for Aid to Jews (the code name was Zegota), and she became one of its most active and accomplished leaders and organizers. Her code name was Jolanta, and she became the one in charge of the Children's Bureau.

The challenge was first of all to help children starving to death in the ghetto (where, at one point, five thousand children were dying every day), and then eventually to get as many children out of the ghetto as possible, passing them on to families who would adopt them, then send them out of the country as their own children, passing them into the hands of religious communities of sisters, especially the Grey Sisters, the Little Servants of the Immaculate Conception, the Franciscans of the Family of Mary, and the order of St. Elizabeth. Sendler would secrete the children in rectories and schools, shuffling them from city to city. It is believed that she saved at least 2,500 children in this way. She alone kept the lists, the names and where the children had been sent. She hid them in jars, burying them in gardens under specific trees so that the Gestapo couldn't find them.

However, on the night of October 20, 1943, the Gestapo did catch up to her. They didn't find the lists, but they imprisoned her in Pawiak, where she was beaten, tortured, and condemned to death. But she was one of the lucky few who had friends who paid a bribe, and she was released. She immediately retrieved her lists in the jars and kept them until the end of the war; then she passed them on to the Jewish Committee so they could begin to find the lost children.

Sendler was later called "the Polish Angel" and honored at Yad Vashem, the Holocaust Martyrs' and Heroes' Remembrance Authority in Jerusalem. Statistics on what happened during the time she was working in the Warsaw Ghetto are appalling:

> Between September 1940 and July 1942, an estimated 100,000 Jewish men, women, and children died in the Warsaw Ghetto. Another 300,000 Jews were sent from there in 1942 to die in the Treblinka concentration camp.[9]

Sendler didn't speak much about why she did what she did — why she put her life in jeopardy day after day. All she would say was that her father had taught her the difference between good people and bad people, and that nothing else mattered. She also commented, "Hitler created hell for all of us in Poland. But the kind of hell he made for the Jews was even greater."[10]

And what she did was organized with hundreds of other people; individuals like her friends, family members, associates, priests, and religious communities made her work and the saving of the children possible. She put into practice what Joan Baez says: "That's all nonviolence is — organized love."

There were others during World War II who refused in their own ways to be a part of the killing and sought to make others aware of what was happening and turn people toward resistance. Sophie Scholl, her brother Hans, and their friends formed a group known as the White Rose. She was twenty-one, a student at the University in Munich. Group members wrote pamphlets and distributed them around the city, quoting theological arguments encouraging resistance and noncompliance with Hitler's programs; they also organized study groups teaching nonviolence and noncooperation. The group was eventually put on trial. This is one of Sophie Scholl's statements during the trial about why they did what they did, and how they saw themselves in the larger history of being Christian (they were primarily Lutherans):

> Everywhere and at all times of greatest trial [people] have appeared, prophets and saints who cherished their freedom, who preached the One God and who with [God's] help brought the people to a reversal of their downward course. Man is free, to be sure, but without the true God he is defenseless against the principle of evil. . . . We will not be silent. We are your bad conscience. The White Rose will not leave you in peace.[11]

The trial was a sham, yet the group members stood before the court and defied the judges. It all went so fast: within a day of their arrest, they were jailed, put through the court-room travesty of a trial and the summoning of their parents, sentenced, and beheaded within the hour after the trial was over.

Sophie Scholl had much in common with Hannah Senesh, a Jewish resistance leader who sought to bring people to freedom and ran messages back and forth across battle lines. Eventually she was captured, tortured, and killed. Just before her execution, she scribbled a poem

122

on a piece of paper called "The Matchstick." It is short — it can be read in the time it takes to light a match and let it burn down to your fingertips. It was the symbol of her life — brief, passionate, bringing light and fire to the truth before being snuffed out.

> *I am your message, Lord. Throw me like a blazing torch into the night,*
> *that all may see and understand what it means to be a disciple.*
> St. Maria Skobtsova, Orthodox nun and martyr, 1891-1945

The sixtieth anniversary of Pax Christi International was celebrated in 2005. Many people know that it was co-founded by two people. They know the name of the bishop, Pierre-Marie Théas, of Montauban in southern France, but many are unaware of the other founder, Marthe Dortel-Claudot, who took the initiative in the endeavor. She taught literature at a school in Agen and was fiercely opposed to what was developing in France. What follows is a description of how she came to found Pax Christi:

> Her moment of inspiration came while she was praying in her parish church on 23 December 1944. With sudden anguish she reflected on what Christmas would be like for the suffering German people. In the following months she felt drawn more and more to pray that Germany would be healed of the spiritual and moral effects of twelve years of Nazi rule.
>
> Encouraged by her parish priest, she invited others to share this prayer of reconciliation. The first to join her were a war widow, the daughter of a deportee, and the local Carmelite community.
>
> Hoping to find a bishop who would endorse her project, Marthe Dortel-Claudot went to see Bishop Théas on 11 March 1945. He was sympathetic and agreed, provided his Archbishop approved. So the next day she visited the Archbishop of Toulouse, and won his support.[12]

The movement grew like wildfire and soon extended to the concepts of world peace and moved beyond prayer into all fields of justice, peace-making, and nonviolent conflict negotiation, working with the victims of conflict and conscientious objectors, and also working in legal areas against war and nationalism. One person, then two or three can start a movement that can spread across all borders and boundaries. Simply put, Pax Christi, the Peace of Christ, proclaims that the core of the Good News of God is "no war," and that being a believer entails working actively against all the issues that can lead to war, and seeking to stop conflict, as well as praying and living a lifestyle of no violence singularly and in communities of faith.

Bits of Crucial Information:
100,000 heartbeats a day in a human body.
100,000 miles of blood cells.
127 million light-sensitive cells in the retina of eyes.
Can distinguish 10,000 smells. . . .

Vs.

As of April 10, 2008, the costs for the Iraq war alone are as follows, with links to where this information can be found:

Dollar Cost:
Total: $510,126,908,796.
Per household: $4,681.
Per person: $1,721.
Daily cost: $341.4 million
(nationalpriorities.org/costofwar)

U.S. Casualties:
Deaths: 4,032
Wounded: between 29,628-100,000
(antiwar.com/casualties)

Iraqi Casualties:
Deaths — 1,197,469
(justforeignpolicy.org/iraq/)[13]

Kathy Kelly is the co-coordinator of Voices for Creative Nonviolence and travels extensively and continually throughout the Middle East, Afghanistan, and other areas of violence and conflict. She shares the life of the people and is, as it were, an ambassador for peace and compassion to them as both an individual and a member of many communities that seek to end the wars and the continuing horrors of an occupied Iraq (she has been to Iraq more than twenty-four times for extended periods), the tensions and escalations in Palestine, especially in the West Bank with Israel; and the horrors in Afghanistan and elsewhere. She seeks to share their experiences, listen to their stories, and suffer the deprivations and losses that they know in their daily lives in an effort to open bridges of communication. Then she returns to the United States and other countries with first-hand and "first-heart" information on what it is like "on the ground" in these wars that are, for the most part, only covered from a tactical and military point of view. For her, all persons in a city bombed, a country devastated are real persons with bones that break, bodies that bleed, hearts that ache, and minds that seek some sort of meaning for what is happening to them and why their lives are filled with such bitterness, hate, grief, and loss. Kathy Kelly visits and speaks in churches and schools, speaks at protests, and gives major addresses to religious/political groups and organizations — to anyone who will listen.

Recently, Joshua McElwee interviewed Kathy (along with Marie Dennis and Liz McAlister, other women who have worked for peace over the last decades) at the School of the Americas watch vigil, which was held 20-22 November 2009 at Ft. Benning, Georgia. She responded to the question "How, day to day, do you find the strength to do your work?" This is a portion of her answer:

> My answer is actually younger people. If I'm in touch with the people whose future is so affected by what my generation has done, then I will work harder to try to offset some of the mistakes that my generation and others before me have put in place. That's sort of what keeps me going. I wouldn't call it guilt, but a sense of being responsible and being with the younger people. Any time I can go to a high school, then I really feel energized. I think: "I'm

not going to walk out on these new people." Also, my memories help me. I'm never going to walk away from an Iraqi woman whose baby was dying in her arms and just say, "Well, it's politically difficult to organize around this issue."[14]

In correspondence with me, Kathy also offered these comments:

I believe that nonviolence can change the world, that the needs of those most impoverished in our world should be our highest priority, and that we should never let inconvenience prevent us from living in accord with our highest values.

Strength, in the sense of real security, comes from communities pulling together in compassion and cooperation. Strength comes from decency. We are made insecure by our criminal assaults on international security and our criminal neglect of the poor at home. Who will educate us to better understand that being seen as a menacing, frightful, and destructive culture, internationally, jeopardizes our security? International law establishes that initiating war, as we did in Iraq and indeed in Afghanistan, is a crime; and in a fundamental sense, for those who wish to live in security, crime does not pay.

Our strength will not come from diversions of desperately needed resources into meaningless destruction and division. Individual Americans, without waiting for help from above, must act to correct these pathologies of American social and political life. We can support and learn from decent and kindly organizers, thinking of Joan Baez's fine description of nonviolence as "organized love." Across the U.S. and the world are communities that extend a hand of friendship to those all too often viewed as expendables. We can donate from our own resources to fight poverty at home and thereby deny these resources as taxable income that our government can employ in causing more despair, poverty, and displacement abroad. And we can build bonds of community and shared purpose, organizing in our neighborhoods, our cities, our schools, our churches, and our workplaces, to build a world wherein no one is left out in the cold.

126

Kathy lives and struggles with personal questions in a very public context of history, political decisions, and military incursions and bombings that impact millions of people. She sides with them physically, being with them because her faith demands it — to mitigate the sufferings of others; to know and live with some of the people who bear the heavy burden and brunt of our wars, our unprovoked attacks, our containment of countries, and our empire-building. Kathy Kelly knows in her heart what Jody Williams is saying. Williams, from Northern Ireland, won the 1997 Nobel Peace Prize for her work in banning land mines. She comments,

> You need a little of this, a dash of that, a sprinkle of salt or whatever, to make a recipe come together and be really good. . . . The same things with peace. . . . You need justice, you need equality, you need human rights and more.[15]

I do not know if Kathy Kelly has ever met or spoken with Jody Williams, but both women share a sense of awe and wonder at human beings — all human beings — and a reverence that leads them to care for their bodies as much as their souls, and to work so that they all might have life, ever more abundantly, and be rescued from the harm that has been and is still being done to them by other Christians or religious people.

All of these women know in their own bodies both the pain and the delight, the terror and the joy, the loss and the possibilities of new life that are the fruits of peace-making and seeking to give birth to a world that is lived with less violence and war than the one we have so often wreaked on others in these past decades. We would echo and resonate with Etty Hillesum's expression of what it means somehow at our deepest roots to be human and to be before God and before one another every moment of our lives:

> A desire to kneel down sometimes pulses through my body, or rather it is as if my body has been meant and made for the act of kneeling. Sometimes, in moments of deep gratitude, kneeling

down becomes an overwhelming urge, head deeply bowed, hands before my face.[16]

This attitude, this undergirding of a spiritual life, and this sense of the sacredness of all life, of every person's body, are shared by those who spend their energies and lives as midwives drawing forth peace from every brutal situation and experience of violence and suffering. Hillesum writes again in her diary — on July 12, 1942 — some lines she titles her "Sunday morning prayer." These words summon us to a relationship with God that is based on the reality around us, the truth of who God is, and the power of what we are called to be as human beings:

> Dear God, these are anxious times. Tonight for the first time I lay in the dark with burning eyes as scene after scene of human suffering passed before me. . . . I shall try to help You, God, to stop my strength from ebbing away, though I cannot vouch for it in advance. But one thing is becoming increasingly clear to me: that You cannot help us, that we help You to help ourselves. And that is all we can manage these days and also all that really matters: we are to safeguard that little of You, God, in ourselves. And perhaps in others as well. Alas, there doesn't seem to be much You Yourself can do about our circumstances, about our lives. Neither do I hold you responsible. You cannot help us, but we must help You and defend your dwelling place inside us to the last. . . .[17]

In spite of the memories of humiliation, I stand with the people of Guatemala. I demand the right to heal and to know the truth. I demand the right to a resurrection.

Dianna Ortiz

Dianna Ortiz, originally from New Mexico, was twenty-eight years old.[18] She was an Ursuline sister, a missionary in San Miguel Acatan, Guatemala. She was a schoolteacher, teaching Mayan children to read and write and to appreciate more deeply their own culture, and to read the Bible in their own language and so to live it more deeply in their own lives and country.

Ortiz recounts what happened to her simply, starkly, without excuses, and blunts the atrocities that she experienced even as she tells the truth about them. She outlines the bare essentials, leaving out pieces too painful to relate, too intimate to share, and too much for anyone listening to her to hear. This is what her book, *The Blindfold's Eye*, is like. It is so truthful, so descriptive, and so reflective that one can read only a few pages at a time — it is a self-examination that makes a reader feel as though she experiences vicariously some of the fear and torture that Ortiz suffered.

In a press conference on 6 May 1996 in the park in front of the White House, she began with these words: "Over five weeks ago, I stood in Lafayette Park, along with other survivors of torture in Guatemala. The tulips were only slips of leaves, patches like open hands. During two of the past five weeks I have fasted, losing twenty-five pounds. In Guatemala, approximately ten people have been tortured since the tulips budded and bloomed."[19]

Ortiz had spoken in public for the first time about what had happened to her on Palm Sunday, 31 March 1996, in that same park. She and many others had just completed a long vigil. They sought to have the United States reveal the documents on Ortiz's torture and the United States' role in the tortures, assassinations, and disappearances that had been occurring in Guatemala over the last thirty years — leaving over 150,000 Guatemalans dead and 45,000 missing. She described the silence of the vigil as not "the silence of complicity, but a silence of commemoration for those who had been tortured, killed, and 'disappeared.'" She spoke of all of them, the survivors of this abuse and those who had died, needing the information that the United States has, and she demanded that it be handed over and made public. She said, "We need and demand this information so that we can heal our wounds, bury our dead, and carry on with our lives."[20]

And then Ortiz told her story. To read the words is one thing; to hear them in her voice is another altogether. But the reading is still very powerful:

Many of you know my story. . . . For a long time I received death threats. Then on November 2, 1989, I was abducted from the backyard of the Posada de Belen retreat center in Antigua by members of the Guatemalan security forces. They took me to a clandestine prison where I was tortured and raped repeatedly. My back and chest were burned more than 111 times with cigarettes. I was lowered into an open pit packed with human bodies — bodies of children, women, and men, some decapitated, some lying face up and caked with blood, some dead, some alive — and all swarming with rats.

After hours of torture, I was returned to a room where the interrogation initially occurred. In this room I met Alejandro, a tall man of light complexion. As my torturers began to rape me again, they said to him, "Hey, Alejandro, come and have some fun." They referred to him as their "boss." Alejandro cursed in unmistakable American English and ordered them to stop, since I was a North American nun and my disappearance had become public.[21]

Ortiz went on to speak of Alejandro, who "rescued her." He helped her get her clothes on, and then he took her to a gray Suzuki jeep, telling her in heavily accented Spanish that he was taking her to the American Embassy and that a friend who would help her to leave the country. On that trip they spoke in fluent English. He kept telling her that he was sorry for what had happened to her, that it was a mistake and she should forgive them and forget about it. If she didn't, he would incriminate her with the tapes, photographs, and video of what had happened and the crimes that she had been forced to participate in. She was threatened by her "rescuer." She ended the press conference with this brutally honest description and cry:

The memories of what I experienced that November day haunt me even now. I can smell the decomposing bodies, disposed of in an open pit. I can see the blood gushing out of the woman's body as I thrust a small machete into her. For you see, I was handed a machete. Thinking that it would be used against me, and at that point in my torture wanting to die, I did not resist. But my torturers put their hands onto the handle, on top of mine. And I had no choice. I was forced to use it against another human being. What I remem-

ber is blood gushing — spurting like a water fountain — and my
screams lost in the cries of the woman.

In spite of the memories of humiliation, I stand with the people
of Guatemala. I demand the right to heal and to know the truth. I
demand the right to a resurrection.[22]

Ortiz's story is unique, as is the story of every survivor of torture.
She has sought to come to grips with what was done to her, what was
taken from her, and how what was done to her body shattered her
mind, her heart, and her soul — and then to fight her way back to living and redeeming her life with others. She is the founder and the current director of Torture Abolition and Survivors Support Coalition International. She is intent on bringing those who torture to justice, to
exposing the lies behind those who use and allow torture and to
changing the statutes on this crime, bringing it completely to an end.

In February 2008, she wrote an open letter as a torture survivor to
all the candidates running for the U.S. presidency, demanding to
know where they stood on the issues, and where they stood on the
Military Commissions Act. Should the U.S. president be allowed to
designate and detain unlawful enemy combatants, including U.S. citi-
zens, without charge? Should the president have the right to decide
what practices constitute torture? And should evidence be admissible
at trial that has been obtained through coercion? Ortiz mentioned
other associated issues — dealing with rape and sexual assault, arrest
on hearsay, habeas corpus, and so on — but she demanded that all
candidates answer clearly what they believe and would legislate and
practice. She posited that an affirmative answer to any of the above
questions made one an advocate of torture. She ended her letter this
way — making the issue of torture central to many other issues:

In the last few years, there has been a significant change in the
amount of conversation about torture — from nearly nothing to
an incessant drumbeat. Sadly, the subject has now become debat-
able. What is the proper way to commit crimes against humanity,
open and above-board or in secret shrouded lies? How much pain
is too much? What kind of brutality leaves a lasting impact? Con-

gress talks on and on, wanting desperately not to answer these questions. How do we know? Because they do not ask those who do know. YOU do not ask torture's survivors. None of you asks us. And some of you even refuse to respond to our calls and letters to meet to dialogue about the issue and its effects.

. . . For those who truly oppose torture, we ask, "When will your actions match your words?" Stop beating about the bush![23]

All of these women, and so many others — the list grows longer with each passing day — seek to do the impossible: redeem and share resurrection with those whose bodies, minds, hearts, and souls have been grievously offended, abused, beaten down, humiliated, imprisoned, and bent to the power and violence of other human beings. They know that one cannot be consoled over certain things; that certain memories cannot be erased — and should not; that certain deeds cry out for justice and to be heard; that certain things are inhuman and not to be tolerated, let alone discussed rationally; that certain actions can never be excused; and that certain actions still can be transformed through grace and the extreme love that bring a human being to forgiving and loving one's enemy, with mercy, yet demanding still that the truth be told, and justice be honored. It's as difficult as giving birth. It is, hopefully, as inevitable as giving birth and believing and acting as though the time is now.

Sources Used in This Chapter

(These are put in the order of the persons mentioned in the text, followed by general information that might be helpful.)

Life in a Jar. This play about Irena Sendler is available on DVD from www.irenasendler.org.

Sophie Scholl. This film of Scholl's story is available on DVD from Ignatius Press (1-800-651-1531).

Blessed Is the Match: The True Story of Hannah Senesh. This DVD is available from www.blessedisthematch.com.

Pax Christi International Newsletter, St. Joseph's, Watford Way, Hendon, London, NW4 4TY. The Web addresses are paxchristi@gn.apc.org and www.paxchristi.org.uk. There is also Pax Christi USA, 532 West Eighth St., Erie, Pa. 16502. The Web addresses are intro@paxchristiusa.org and www.paxchristiusa.org.

Voices for Creative Nonviolence: Go to info@vcnv.org.

New Internationalist magazine, North American edition: Go to friend@newint.org.

International Center on Nonviolent Conflict: Go to icnc@nonviolent-conflict.org.

"Speaking of Faith." Access at newsletter@speakingoffaith.org for weekly presentations and interviews with Krista Tippett. Also see her book, *Why Religion Matters and How to Talk about It.*

AlterNet: Go to www.alternet.org.

Independent Catholic News: Go to ifor@indcatholicnewscom.

Dianna Ortiz. "A Letter from a Torture Survivor to Those Seeking the Democratic and Republican Nominations for President in 2008," *Tikkun,* January/February 2008, pp. 44-45.

Rose Marie Berger and Julie Polter. "Sister Dianna Ortiz: Death's Dance Broken," in *Cloud of Witnesses,* ed. Jim Wallis and Joyce Hollyday, rev. ed., pp. 37-42. Maryknoll, N.Y.: Orbis Books, 2005.

Dianna Ortiz. *The Blindfold's Eye: My Journey from Torture to Truth.* Maryknoll, N.Y.: Orbis Books, 2002.

Eduardo Galeano. *Voices of Time: A Life in Stories.* Trans. Mark Fried. Metropolitan Books. New York: Henry Holt & Co., 2006.

Chapter 8

Paracletes and Advocates for Justice

The greatness of a community is most accurately measured by the compassionate actions of its members, a heart of grace, and a soul generated by love.

Coretta Scott King

Looking at the title of this chapter, one might wonder, "What is a paraclete?" In a court of law, "advocate" is the term used to describe someone who defends another. "Paraclete" is both a legal and a theological term for one who stands at your side, in close proximity, a companion on your way, especially when you stand in jeopardy or need an ally — someone who will vouch for you, stand up for you, and believe in you. In Christianity, the Advocate and the Paraclete is the Holy Spirit, the Spirit of the Risen Lord, the Spirit of Truth, given to believers as their first gift as they stand in the world and seek to speak the Truth, stand up for the Truth, and speak on behalf of others in their defense. It is a gift given for others that often puts one in the position of being the subject of hatred, wrath, and violence when other people are discouraged or kept from injustice and the ill treatment of those they intend to harm, use, or abuse.

But it is also a gift that is given to be passed on to others, shared, taught, and extended. In the second book of Kings, Elijah passes on this prophetic and truthful gift to his follower, Elisha, by dropping his cloak so that Elisha might pick it up as Elijah leaves — a double portion of Spirit to speak the Truth to the nation and its leaders. It is then Elisha who wields Elijah's mantle like a sword that cuts through all things to reveal the truth (2 Kings 2). And at the end of the Gospel of Luke, Jesus tells his friends and followers to go into the city of Jerusalem and wait there together "until you are clothed with power from on high" (Luke 24:49). This is the gift of the Spirit of Truth — the mantle of Jesus that will be given to them, to all who come to serve the Truth. It is the gift and the presence of these and so many women in the world. Part of the marvel of this gift is how it is practiced, and the diversity with which each wields the mantle and expresses this Spirit. The gift is found in ancient and ever-new traditions and in human beings. There are many paracletes loose in the world!

There is a legend from China called "The Beautiful Warrior." There are many versions of this story (e.g., a children's book by Emily Arnold McCully from the Wu Mei Kung Fu Foundation), but all of them concentrate on the elements of mind, body, and spirit energy that are needed for the martial art of kung fu. Originally, kung fu was not about defeating or even overcoming your enemy but first showing that the other had no power over you. From that position, many options became available. This is a short version of "The Beautiful Warrior" as I tell it.

Once upon a time, a baby girl was born inside the Forbidden City during the reign of the last Ming emperor (around 1640). Her father watched her before naming her. She had a steady gaze, and so he named her Jing Yong, meaning "Quiet Courage." From the beginning he decided to train her in the five pillars of learning, as he would a son: art, literature, music, medicine, and the martial arts. She soon knew her qi (vital energy) and learned quickly that softness can prevail over hardness and a yielding force can master a brute one. She grew up quickly, and her mother despaired of ever finding a husband who would marry a girl so trained and sure of herself. "She will find her own path," her father insisted.

But one day, Manchu warriors entered the Forbidden City, and the Ming dynasty was ended. Jing Yong was separated from her parents and left to fend for herself. In her studies she had learned about the

135

monastery of the Shoalin, where monks had practiced and taught kung fu for over a thousand years, and she set off to find it. When she reached the monastery, she asked for permission to live with the monks. She won entrance by easily defeating a monk who challenged her kung fu skills. Her head was shaved, and she was given robes and a new name: Wu Mei, meaning "Beautiful Warrior." She became a nun, begging in the streets daily and living with a calm focus. Many came to study with her, but she taught only the ones who did not want to harm or overcome others.

One day while Wu Mei was begging, a young girl who sold beans, Mingyi Wang, delivered bean cakes to one of the magistrates' houses. It was a huge order, and she left with a purse that she knew would be her dowry. But suddenly there were robbers in front of her. She looked around, desperate, but there was only this small nun begging at the end of the street. The next moment a great wind sucked at them — the nun was concentrating on them and breathing out one breath! She seemed to grow larger; when her feet thundered, all the robbers were on the ground. Then the nun seemed tiny again. And she sent Mingyi home.

But Mingyi would return all too soon. Bandits came to her village, and once the leader saw Mingyi, he decided he wanted to marry her. Mingyi despaired, pleaded with her parents, but they were terrified. She'd have to marry him — what could they do against him and his gang? Mingyi rushed to the monastery and found Wu Mei.

"You must kill him and save me!" Mingyi begged.

But Wu Mei only used her kung fu to save lives, not to take them. But she had an idea. "Tell him you need a year. Then come here, and I will teach you all you need to know to best him. At the end of the year, challenge him — but if he can best you at kung fu, you will marry him."

Poor Mingyi was in despair. "How can I ever best him — he's huge!"

"Trust me," replied Wu Mei. "It's the only way."

What else could Mingyi do? Off she went and laid out the rules to the bandit. He laughed — "What a joke!" — but he agreed to wait.

Wu Mei and Mingyi had a year. Wu Mei began by telling her new student that kung fu was a lifetime study and practice, but that she would teach her the basics. It would be hard, but she must obey.

For the first lesson, Wu Mei took her to a pond of still water. "Make your mind as calm as the water," Wu Mei instructed. All Mingyi could see was her troubled face.

For the second lesson, Wu Mei took her to a rushing stream. "See how the water finds the path of least resistance. Water is soft yet wears away rock."

For the third lesson, Wu Mei took her to a bamboo forest. "Look at the bamboo. When the wind blows, it bends and does not break. When the wind quiets, bamboo stands up upright."

Mingyi was growing impatient. "When do I fight?"

Wu Mei answered, "You are learning now."

This was the first week's work. Then Wu Mei took Mingyi to the practice courtyard. There were five wooden posts stuck in the ground. Wu Mei jumped up on one and then moved to the next one gracefully, dancing. Mingyi got up and fell off. "Concentrate," instructed Wu Mei.

This work took many months. Eventually Mingyi was graceful, quick, and agile. She and Wu Mei would both move back and forth, each watching the other, learning where the other would move next.

"What are you learning?" Wu Mei asked.

Mingyi answered, "My feet are like roots, but my body moves, swings. I must concentrate, flow."

"Now you are ready for the hardest part," Wu Mei told her. "Meditation." They sat and sat and sat — it was the hardest discipline of all. When Mingyi twitched, squirmed, and brushed the flies away, Wu Mei promptly rapped her lightly with a stick.

One day, when the year was almost up, the bandit decided to spy on them. He saw his bride-to-be sitting on the ground, doing nothing, and being lightly struck now and then by a nun. He laughed to himself . . . this would be fun. But Mingyi was learning how to be so still that she could sense what her opponent would do before he did it. She was to use his strength and force to defeat him.

One morning, it was time for Mingyi to go. "The time has flown by!" she exclaimed. "Am I ready?"

"Yes," said Wu Mei, nodding. "Just remember that you are not out to overpower him or harm him — only to show that he has no power over you."

Back in her village, Mingyi stood before Ling, the leader of the bandits. His gang was watching and making fun — in fact, the whole village was watching. Everything for the wedding was ready. *This is going to be fun,* Mingyi thought to herself.

She concentrated. She flowed like water. And she waited for Ling to move. When he threw his weight at her, she wasn't there! Again and again Ling tried this and failed. He started panting. When he went to punch her, he punched air. Eventually Ling yelled, "I'm going to squash you like a bean cake!" And everyone roared.

Now he was growing more careful — and more tired. It was like a dance. Mingyi would move like the wind, then she'd stand still like a crane, then she'd feint like a turtle with her head, then she'd move like the wind again. Finally Ling's own force and uncontrolled strength undid him. And Mingyi gathered her qi and went over to him. She lifted him up off the ground over her head, and then she dropped him back on the ground.

Ling's gang was stunned. "That's all right," he said loudly. "Who would want to marry her anyway? I can have anyone I want." And he got up and left with his gang.

Mingyi's mother didn't know whether to laugh or cry. She was glad that the bandit would not be her son-in-law, but who now would marry her daughter when the story got around?

There was a celebration in the village. There was no wedding, but the people were now free of the bandit and his gang. Wu Mei had come to see her student. Mingyi bowed deeply to her master and asked permission to come to the monastery and really learn how to concentrate — not to fight but to live and to be aware of everything around her, mastering herself and living in harmony with all of the universe.

Wu Mei smiled and said, "Remember, this is the study and work of a lifetime. It is a way of living and being with all things."

Then the two women bowed to each other, and they went home to the monastery.

"The Beautiful Warrior" is a story steeped in Chinese culture that functions as a basic introduction to the art of kung fu — which literally means "human effort." It is an art of the mind, a discipline that does not depend on size or strength or even bravery, and certainly not on force. Kung fu developed from Chan (Zen) Buddhism around the year 600 as a series of exercises meant to train the mind and steady the heart and body for the practice of meditation. Only later did this develop into a form of challenge between uneven forces.

This story lays the foundation for looking at the women in this chapter: women whose lives have been dedicated to advocacy for justice on behalf of others in politics, in courts of law and tribunals. They are Buddhist, Russian Orthodox, Christian, Catholic — and all share a devotion to the rights of others. All practice a discipline of nonviolence. Some have been persecuted; some have paid for their devotion to others with their lives.

One woman died at ninety-two on October 24, 2005. She had lived through segregation in the South, a legal system that humiliated her people, robbed them of dignity, and insulted them daily. She was arrested, jailed, and threatened with death. Those who supported her and rallied around her had their houses fire-bombed. And she and her husband lost their jobs. All because of a single decision she made when she was on the way home from work one night. She was sitting in a seat on a public bus in Montgomery, Alabama, on December 1, 1955 — and she just decided not to give it up to a white man. "I was tired of giving in," she said. In a posthumous editorial, the *Washington Post* said, "A single act, a bold stroke, by a dignified African-American fifty years ago dramatically altered the course of American history. Rosa Parks is a name for the ages."[1]

Her arrest sparked a protest movement and changed her life forever, drawing her deep into the public struggle that became the civil rights movement in the South and spread not just across America but demanded that people everywhere look to their consciences and to their laws and prejudices. In a sense, she was midwife to the movement, opening the way for Martin Luther King Jr. to begin the struggle for change in earnest. Years after that history-changing day, she wrote, "If our lives demonstrate that we are peaceful, humble, and trusted, this is recognized by others. If our lives demonstrate something else, that will be noticed too."

Hers was one moment, one decision, one act of exhaustion after years of suffering and "putting up with it." But it was a moment at the right time — it was 1955. Rosa Parks was forty-two, married with no children, and an active member of the NAACP. In another piece in the *Washington Post,* Will Haygood remembers her this way:

> For the rest of her life, Parks gave the impression that her nation-altering protest would have occurred even if there had been no TV cameras, no radio, no newspapers. Her move seemed deep as Gospel and in the end, timeless. A declaration both simple and eloquent: I am a lady. And I'd like to remain in my seat, please.[2]

Another black woman, a sharecropper's daughter who was married to a tractor driver on a neighboring plantation, couldn't have her own children. She and her husband adopted two daughters: Dorothy, who was given to them at birth by a single mother, and Virgie, who they got when the child was about five; she had been badly burned. This black woman was barren — not like the matriarchs in the Bible, she would say, but because of men. She'd gone into a clinic in Mississippi to have a small uterine cyst removed, and without her knowledge or consent, the doctor had given her a hysterectomy. She grieved her whole life over what was taken from her.

Fannie Lou Hamer worked in the fields for over twenty years. Later she would say, "Sometimes I be working in the fields, and I get so tired, I say to the people picking cotton with us, 'Hard as we have to work for nothing, there must be some way we can change this.'"[3] And in August 1962, the Freedom Riders arrived in town to help people prepare and register to vote for the first time. Hamer went to a rally where Jim Forman of the Student Nonviolent Coordinator Committee (the SNCC) spoke, quoting Matthew 16:3 on "discerning the signs of the times." Now it was time to register and vote. Fannie Lou Hamer was forty-five years old when she went to vote. But she failed a test where she had to copy out and interpret an obscure reference in the constitution of Mississippi. She failed often, but she took the test every month and finally passed it over a year later. And then her life's work began.

Hamer started working for the SNCC — in the fields with folks by day and in churches at night. There were repercussions: she and her husband lost their land on the plantation and their jobs and started getting death threats. But Hamer was undeterred. She became a preacher and a singer. She traveled the country, registering people to vote and working for the rights of blacks, seeking to give them an identity and a self-respect so that they could obtain what was theirs by law and live with dignity. She spoke to white audiences too in the North, describing the desperate conditions that was life for most black Americans in the South. She was not always well-received. She was beaten — once so badly that she suffered kidney damage and permanent impairment of her vision.

And Fannie Lou Hamer sang — she sang praise and intercession, and she sang her way through life, to freedom, and others joined her in song. Some say that her caucusing and working for black voting rights was important, but it was her singing that everyone remembered and that moved people most to action. And it was her singing that somehow infuriated people too. A story is told about her and others who got off a bus in Winona, Mississippi. Hamer was beaten badly, and then she and the others were told to just leave. But they stayed because they were sure that if they left, they'd be killed and dumped in some river, and no one would ever find them. Because they stayed, they were jailed. Charles Marsh, author of *God's Long Summer*, describes what happened next:

Mrs. Hamer's suffering and humiliation left her with the certainty that death was imminent. There was no singing at this nightfall. But then the next day something happened that slowly transformed the killing despair of the jail and dispersed the power of death. "When you're in a brick cell, locked up, and haven't done anything to anybody but still you're locked up there, well, sometimes words just begin to come to you and you begin to sing," she said. Song broke free. Mrs. Hamer sang:

Paul and Silas was bound in jail, let my people go!
Had no money for to go their bail, let my people go!
Paul and Silas began to shout, let my people go!
Jail doors open and they walked out, let my people go!

141

Fannie Lou Hamer's songs raised up the lowly and brought down the powerful. She remained barren all her life, but her singing conceived for an entire nation what Abraham Lincoln called "a new birth of freedom."[4]

She was a tough woman, faithful and determined. At one point, when times were worse than usual, she would tell people that she wondered every day when she got up if she'd still be alive when darkness came. And she said, "If I fall, I'll fall five feet four inches forward in the fight for freedom. I'm not backing off that, and no one will have to cover the ground I walk as far as freedom is concerned."[5]

These two women stand on the shoulders of many who went before them, like Sojourner Truth, born a slave in 1797 in Hurley, New York. Her given name was Isabella, which she laid down at the age of forty-six, when she became a prophet and preacher. She spoke Dutch, and she taught herself English. She was the ninth child in her family, but she never knew her brothers and sisters — they were all sold to others, as she was, over and over again. From the beginning she talked to God — her mother taught her to — and she would begin many of her speeches and sermons with these words: "Children, listen to me! I talk to God, and God talks to me!" She said that it was God who heard her cries and her prayers in despair and suffering, and it was God who taught her and told her that one day she'd be free. She was married to another slave and had five children, but one day, she just walked away — "stole away," as she'd say — taking the youngest and leaving the others behind. She worked in New York as a servant, but decided that God was calling her to the ministry of telling the truth, traveling up and down this land, showing people their sins, being a sign unto them and preaching from the Scriptures, great portions of which she learned by heart. She was a sojourner telling the truth.

She worked for the abolition of slavery, but also for the women's movement — she didn't want black men to be masters of black women — and said that slavery and women's place in society were bound tight together. She believed that slavery would be abolished, and she lived to see the Thirteenth Amendment to the Constitution passed on December 12, 1865. She had lived through the war and had worked with black soldiers in the Union Army during the war and with refugees in Washington, D.C., after the war. She died at eighty-six, on November 26, 1883.

She was a whip with her words and her wit, sharp as a tack, smart and deft in her phrasing and her repartee in public. This piece is perhaps the one she is most remembered for:

> I have plowed and planted and gathered into barns, and no man could head me — and ain't I a woman? I have born'd five childrun and seen 'em mos' all sold off into slavery, and when I cried out with a mother's grief, none but Jesus heard — and ain't I a woman? . . . Den dat little man in black dar, he say women can't have as much rights as man, 'cause Christ warn' a woman. Whar did your Christ come from? Whar did your Christ come from? From God and a woman! Man had nothing to do with him![6]

But Sojourner Truth's words about death that have appeared on cards, posters, and banners say more about her soul. She spoke these words, it is said, only a few days before she died: "I'm not going to die, honey. I'm going home like a shooting star!"

If you love Jesus Christ more than you fear human judgment, then you will not only speak of compassion, but act with it. Compassion means seeing your friend and your enemy in equal need, and helping both equally. It demands that you seek and find the stranger, the broken, the prisoner, and comport him and offer him your help. Herein lies the holy compassion of God that causes the devil much distress.

Mechthild of Magdeburg

There are three women from Latin America whose hearts and lives could be a braid tying the people of the Americas together: Dolores Huerta, Digna Ochoa y Plácido, and Rigoberta Menchú Tum.

Dolores Huerta, who is almost eighty, was one of the co-founders — with Cesar Chavez and Philip Vera Cruz — of the United Farm Workers in the 1960s. She worked tirelessly to start and complete the grape boycott that culminated in a new contract and a victory for the farm workers and the labor movement. She has worked at community organizing for most of her life, but has also worked with those working in health-care facilities for the elderly. She believes that community organizing processes and techniques should be used in government agencies and legal systems as well, so that the people who are the majority and in the most need have their agendas met first. When asked who influenced her, she talks of her mother and other strong women and later women who befriended her in society. She loves to tell people this story:

> One former organizer — President Barack Obama — told her, "I stole your slogan." Huerta's phrase, "Si, se puede!" which galvanized the farm workers' movement, translates into English as, "Yes, we can."[7]

She now works for her own foundation — the Dolores Huerta Foundation in Bakersfield, California — concentrating on the issues of preventive health care and the coordinating of health facilities and promoting the elderly as gifts to society that are needed at this crucial time. They offer the gifts of wisdom, experience, the cultures of color, intergenerational communication, and a rich variety of work and religious/personal experiences.

A picture of Huerta at the Latino Inaugural Ball in January 2008 shows a radiant woman with a soft smile on her face. Her open countenance reveals wisdom, hope, and a long faithfulness and suffering gathered together and held with grace.

Rigoberta Menchú Tum belongs to the K'iche'-Maya ethnic group of Guatemala. In 1992 she received the Nobel Peace Prize for her work on behalf of and with the indigenous people there during the five-decades-long civil war. She worked in Guatemala but also around the world, publicizing the horrors that her people were living through. She calls it genocide — the deaths of more than 160,000 indigenous people — 83 percent of whom were killed in the civil war, most by the Guatemalan military. After she lost her family to them, she fled to Mexico in 1981, and now she travels and speaks extensively around the world, because so few of those responsible for the atrocities have been held accountable. In 1999 the United Nations Truth Commission documented and reported that the military was responsible for 93 percent of the human rights violations committed during the long war. This backs up the findings of Nunca Mas ("Never Again"), the independent truth commission of the Catholic Church. But instead of being called to judgment, most of the guilty were given amnesty.

Recently, Menchú gave a talk at the University of Massachusetts in Boston. She spoke about the United Nations Declaration on the Rights of Indigenous Peoples, and called on people — especially lawyers, students, judges, and politicians — to put this text into practice and use it to undo the harm that has been done to so many indigenous people worldwide. In tears, she pleaded, "My entire life I will fight against impunity. It's very important to know that although peace agreements say wonderful things, wonderful things were not done." Besides demanding that past actions be brought to public judgment, Menchú spoke of her present concerns in Guatemala and among the indigenous peoples — especially the situation of children suffering from malnutrition, and the sad fact that 95 percent of women still give birth with no professional access to medicine or health care. Menchú currently serves as the president of a Mexican pharmaceutical company whose mission is to offer inexpensive generic medicines to those in need.

Her autobiography — *I, Rigoberta Menchú* — is both controversial and engaging. It opens up the world of the past fifty years in Guatemala to the minds and hearts of those outside the country. She realizes that some people would like her to be permanently silenced: "Many people would have wanted me to die [already]." That shadow is still with her, along with the memories and the losses of her family. And yet she stands, dressed in her colorful clothes spun of thousands of years of tradition, and speaks of how to live and change the present. Her story, like Dolores Huerta's, is not over yet.

Sadly, the story of Digna Ochoa y Plácido is over. She was born in 1964 in Veracruz, Mexico, into a family deeply involved in human rights — the struggle to secure clean drinking water, land rights for the poor and the workers, and basic access to transportation for their crops. Her experience with the dark side of the struggle began far too early. Her father was arrested, jailed, tortured, and "disappeared." She says, "My father's suffering led me to do something for those suffering injustice, because I saw it in my father's flesh."[8]

Digna Ochoa became a nun and got a law degree and then began her practice. Her first case involved defending peasants who were illegally detained by the police and tortured. And immediately she experienced what she would be up against if she continued: she received death threats, and then was kidnapped and tortured for over a month. She escaped, hiding for a month while her supporters, friends, and fellow lawyers — mostly women — filed a criminal complaint on her behalf; then she was "released." When she was interviewed by Kerry Kennedy Cuomo about her ordeal, she told her,

> The worst was when they said they were holding my father. I knew what my father had suffered, and I didn't want him to relive that. The strongest torture is psychological. Though they also gave me electric shocks and put mineral water up my nose, nothing compared to the psychological torture.

Because of the threats and her worry about what might happen to the rest of her family, she left Veracruz for Mexico City, where she studied human rights law. She then took on two very controversial cases when she worked for the Miguel Agustin Pro Juárez Human Rights Centre. (The center was named after a priest who was executed in Mexico at the beginning of the last century during the persecution of the Catholic Church.) Digna Ochoa's first case involved defending some of the "alleged" members of the Zapatista insurgency in Chiapas in southern Mexico; her second case involved defending Rodolfo Montiel and Teodoro Cabrera, anti-logging environmentalists in the state of Guerrero. (Later, this case was also taken up by the Sierra Club in the United States.) For her participation in the defense of these two men, Digna Ochoa was again kidnapped and beaten, and warned about what would happen to her if she remained on this case. She was released in August 1999, but the death threats came — to her office, to her home. In October, thugs broke into her house, tied her to a chair, beat her, opened a gas line in her home, and left her to die. But she managed to free herself.

Amnesty International recognized her commitment to the rights of the indigenous, poor peasants, and those struggling to protect land and water in their home communities. At that point Digna Ochoa moved to Washington, D.C., and began to work with the Center for Justice and International Law. But in early 2001 she felt she needed to return to her first love and her life's work, so she went back to Mexico City. Several months later, on October 19, 2001, Digna Ochoa was found shot to death in her office. She was thirty-seven years old. Even in death, they would not leave her alone: in July 2003, a special commission investigated her death and declared that it was a suicide. In February 2005, another Mexico City court ordered that the investigation into her death be re-opened because of the outcry and outrage that it provoked in the human rights community worldwide. There has been no word, no vindication yet. Her legacy is what she said and what she did, the cases she fought for and the people she worked for. In her words: "It's injustice that motivates us to do something, to take risks, knowing if we don't, things will remain the same."

It is not easy for a people conditioned by fear under the iron rule of the principle that might is right to free themselves from the enervating miasma of fear. Yet even under the most crushing state machinery, courage rises up again and again, for fear is not the natural state of civilized man.

Aung San Suu Kyi, *Freedom from Fear*

Aung San Suu Kyi (pronounced Ong San Soo Chee) is perhaps the best-known of the women described in this chapter. This is the way her birth announcement reads: "Born June 19, 1945, Aung San Suu Kyi in Rangoon, Burma [now Myanmar]." "Aung San" was for her father, "Suu" for her grandmother, and "Kyi" for her mother. Aung San Suu Kyi's father, a general, is one of Myanmar's foremost national heroes, having fought Japanese invaders during World War II and later helping to secure Burma's independence from England.

Her life followed a simple pattern. She graduated from Oxford with majors in philosophy, politics, and economics. She married Michael Aris on January 1, 1972, and moved to Bhutan, where her husband tutored the royal family. (She and her husband later returned to Britain and had two sons.) In 1988, Burma erupted with student movements and demonstrations in opposition to the military junta that had ruled since 1962. The uprising was quashed with brutal violence. At this point, Suu Kyi returned to lead an opposition movement. Her message grew out of her Buddhist beliefs and practice: unity, discipline, and love. That became not only a slogan but also a source of hope throughout the country, giving her movement — the National League for Democracy — momentum and power across many sectors of society that recognized the Buddhist ideals.

But in May 1989, Tiananmen Square erupted across the international news, and Suu Kyi was placed under house arrest by the military junta. This would be her life, more or less, until the present — more than twenty years' confinement. In 1990 Burma held elections, and Suu Kyi's movement gained 80 percent of the seats in the assembly, and she was elected the first prime minister in Burma since 1962. But the military ignored the election results, kept her imprisoned, and set up the SLORC (State Law and Order Restoration Council) to run the country — the military junta. After that, Burma became one of the most notorious places in the world for human rights abuses, disappearances, the closure of universities and colleges, and the destruction of the economic system (the poor lived in misery while the military enjoyed ostentatious wealth and excess). And Suu Kyi was imprisoned in her neighborhood, cut off from everyone but a servant who lived with her.

She became the symbol of the nation of Burma and all those who hoped for democracy, and she counseled patience, non-violence, persistence, and working for justice. In 1999 she was awarded the Nobel Peace Prize, and her son accepted it on her behalf. (At this point the SLORC had renamed the country Myanmar, but her son did not use that name in his remarks.) Her son dedicated the prize not only to his mother but also to all of Burma. He said, "Theirs is the prize, and theirs will be the eventual victory in Burma's long struggle for peace, freedom, and democracy." Then he added,

"Speaking as [Suu Kyi's] son, however, I would add that I personally believe that by her own dedication and personal sacrifice she has come to be a worthy symbol through whom the plight of all the people of Burma may be recognized."

Suu Kyi's life continued on, and she lost weight — it is thought that the junta was slowly starving her to death, rationing her food. No one visited. In 1999, her husband died in London; she hadn't seen him for four years. She knew that if she left to attend his funeral, she would not be allowed back into Burma — and the military would be delighted if that happened. So she chose to stay.

And she continues to stay. Some call it a stalemate between the military and one woman, with the majority of people standing in solidarity with her. She is allowed out for short periods of time and then, under any pretext possible, she is re-arrested and reconfined. She has been confined now for more than ten of the last fifteen years. Václav Havel, who nominated her for the Nobel Prize, said this — and it still remains true: "She has refused to be bribed into silence by permanent exile. Under house arrest, she has lived in truth. She is an outstanding example of the power of the powerless."

In 2005, Aung San Suu Kyi turned sixty, and she is still deprived of her freedom today (the only Nobel Prize laureate in that position). She has been awarded numerous degrees of honor in absentia — from, among others, the Université Catholique de Louvain in Belgium. In awarding her the degree, they said,

> For years, Aung San Suu Kyi has been calling upon us to support the nonviolent struggle of her people. "Please use your liberty to promote ours" is her constant message. Our liberty can indeed serve hers.
>
> Today, calling for release is no longer enough. But to support her, we must now take action. For means of action do exist. Aung San Suu Kyi and the Burmese democrats in exile have been asking us for years to take three practical steps: economic sanctions, an intervention by the UN Security Council, and greater vigilance from Southeast Asian countries. There is no better way of supporting Aung San Suu Kyi's struggle than by doing everything we can

to achieve these three goals. For it should be remembered that Aung San Suu Kyi has been the only legitimate representative of the Burmese people since 1990.[9]

Just recently Suu Kyi's house arrest has been extended yet again, on a pretext that she harbored someone in her house — a mentally unstable man from the United States who swam across a lagoon in the back of her house; though she pleaded with him to leave, he stayed overnight. She was taken to trial and condemned again. Again she stares down the junta — her own personal history is intimately interwoven with the history of all the Burmese people who have rebelled against those who have suppressed them, enslaved them, impoverished them, and sought to drown out the cry for democracy and freedom.

Some people consider her story a tragedy, others a continuing triumph of enduring faithfulness and adherence to Buddhist principles of right living and nonviolence. Many refer to Suu Kyi as the "Gandhi of Burma." She continues to encourage her people to use nonviolent tactics and peaceful resistance, both in their daily lives and in any political demonstrations and actions against the military. At her last verdict (when she was turning sixty-four), she said,

> For millennia women have dedicated themselves almost exclusively to the task of nurturing, protecting, and caring for the young and the old, striving for the conditions of peace that favor life as a whole. . . . The education and empowerment of women throughout the world cannot fail to result in a more caring, tolerant, just, and peaceful life for all.

To conclude this powerful story, I offer a few short selections from *The Voice of Hope,* a book-long series of interviews with Suu Kyi by Alan Clements:

> AC: What is the core quality at the center of your movement?
> ASSK: Inner strength. It's the spiritual steadiness that comes from the belief that what you are doing is right, even if it doesn't bring you immediate concrete benefits. It's the fact that you are

doing something that helps to shore up your spiritual powers. It's very powerful.

AC: Are you old-fashioned?

ASSK: Well, talking about morality, right and wrong, love and kindness, is considered rather old-fashioned these days, isn't it? But after all, the world is spherical. Perhaps the whole thing will come around again, and maybe I'm ahead of the times.

AC: I'd like to read the final few lines from your essay, "Towards a True Refuge . . .": "The darkness had always been there but the light was new. Because it is new it has to be tended with care and diligence. Even the smallest light cannot be extinguished by all the darkness in the world because darkness is merely the absence of light. But a small light cannot dispel acres of encircling gloom. It needs to grow stronger, and people need to accustom their eyes to the light to see it as benediction rather than pain. We are so much in need of a brighter world which will offer adequate refuge to all its inhabitants." What does the light refer to?

ASSK: Light means that you see a lot of things that you don't want to see, as well as things that you want to see. If there's light, obviously you see everything, so you have to face a lot of things that are both undesirable and desirable. You have to learn to live and cope with the light, with seeing rather than not seeing. A lot of people who commit injustices don't see what they don't want to see. They're blind to the injustice of their own actions. They only see what justifies them in doing what they have done, refusing to see what reflects badly on them. It's the story of SLORC . . . not daring to face the complete picture, that people are fed up with the situation, they are tired of poverty, corruption, aimlessness, and stupidity. But the authorities don't want to see the truth.

[This is Suu Kyi's last line in the interview, a few sentences later.]

Burma should be helped at a time when help is needed. And one day we hope to be ourselves in a position to help others in need.[10]

There are so many other women who could be included with these women who have worked for justice and human rights for their people, for the truth to be told, for a verdict that lays bear the suffering and calls for an apology, for forgiveness, reconciliation, and a just response to what has happened.

There are, for instance, the three women who were the founders of the Mothers of the Plaza de Mayo in Buenos Aires at the end of 1977. (Actually, there were five altogether: Esther Balestrino, Maria Ponce, Azucena Villaflor, and two nuns, Alice Domon and Leonie Duquet.) They had all disappeared, and the government slandered them, saying they were prostitutes working in Mexico. There is a terrible story that cuts like a knife against their disappearance:

A Kiss Opened the Doors to Hell

The kiss was the signal of betrayal, just as in the Gospels: "Whosoever I kiss, that same is the one." In Buenos Aires at the end of 1977, the Blond Angel kissed, one by one, the three founders of the Mothers of the Plaza de Mayo as well as the nuns. And the earth swallowed them. Spokesmen for the dictatorship denied holding the mothers and said the sisters were in Mexico working as prostitutes.

Later on it came out: all of them, mothers and sisters alike, had been tortured and thrown, still alive, from an airplane into the sea.

And the Blond Angel's identity came out too. The papers published a photograph of Captain Alfredo Astiz, his head bowed, surrendering to the English, and despite his beard and cap he was recognized. It was the end of the Falklands War, and he had not fired a shot. He was a specialist in another sort of heroism.[11]

Another remarkable woman is Anna Politkovskaya, a Russian reporter and investigative journalist. In October 2006 she was murdered outside her apartment for the stories she filed on Vladimir Putin's Russia. She described his crackdown on dissidents; his convincing the Duma to give him power to appoint previously elected regional leaders, ending the near-autonomy of the provinces and their ability to protest Kremlin policy; and his jailing of scholars and anyone who opposed him politically. She also suggested that he was behind the murder of human rights activist Nicolai Girenko.

Politkovskaya's diaries were published after her death, and they reveal even more of what Russia is like behind the media-controlled façade. In these pages it becomes clear that she believes that Russia has reverted back to a Soviet-style system in which the individual counts for little, if anything. In one of her last entries, she writes,

> In private [my friends] warn that I will simply be killed if I tell the truth. I am not afraid of this terrorist regime. . . . Our children must grow up free people.[12]

And Politkovskaya's close friend, Natalia Estemirova, was probably the most famous human rights campaigner. The Chechnya-based head of Memorial, Russia's oldest human rights group, was kidnapped from her home in Chechnya and killed. Her body was later found dumped on the main road; there were two bullets in her head and chest. It was July 2009, just three years after Politkovskaya's murder. She was fifty. The two had worked together on many incidents and had been investigating human rights abuses in Chechnya.

Allison Gill, director of Human Rights Watch in Russia, declared, "I have no doubt her killing was to silence her." Estemirova left behind a fifteen-year-old daughter who talks about her mother working in an old building with no electricity or running water. Christiane Amanpour wrote about the challenges her fellow journalist faced:

> I did not know her personally, but I know what drove her. She was a woman who struggled for justice, a mother who was forced to balance love for her daughter with the dangerous duty she shouldered.[13]

Perhaps the best way to end this chapter is with another woman's words, those of Brazilian poet Gabriela Torres Barbosa: "I defy the statistics. But I do not want to do this on my own. I want to be joined by all the other excluded."

Sources Used in This Chapter

Danny Duncan Collum. "Fannie Lou Hamer: Stepping Out into Freedom." In *Cloud of Witnesses*, ed. Jim Wallis and Joyce Hollyday, pp. 90-101. Maryknoll, N.Y.: Orbis Books, 2006.

Nicholas Dristof and Sheryl WuDunn. *Half the Sky: Turning Oppression into Opportunity for Women Worldwide*. New York: Alfred A. Knopf, 2009.

Robert Ellsberg. "Sojourner Truth: Abolitionist Preacher (1797-1883)." In *Blessed among All Women: Women Saints, Prophets, and Witnesses for Our Time*. New York: Crossroad, 2005.

Eduardo Galeano. *Mirrors: The Story of Almost Everyone*. Trans. Mark Fried. New York: Nation Books, 2009.

Joyce Hollyday. "Sojourner Truth: A Pillar of Fire." In *Cloud of Witnesses*, ed. Jim Wallis and Joyce Hollyday, pp. 110-18. Maryknoll, N.Y.: Orbis Books, 2006.

Aung San Suu Kyi. *Freedom from Fear*. Rev. ed. New York: Penguin Books, 1995.

Alice Leuchtag. "Fannie Lou Hamer and the Mississippi Freedom Democratic Party." *Z* magazine, July/August 2008, pp. 18-21.

Charles Marsh. *God's Long Summer: Stories of Faith and Civil Rights*, pp. 20-22. Princeton, N.J.: Princeton University Press, 1997.

Rigoberta Menchú. *I, Rigoberta Menchú: An Indian Woman in Guatemala*. Ed. Elisabeth Burgos-Debray, trans. Ann Wright. London: Verso, 1984.

Anna Politkovskaya. *A Russian Diary: A Journalist's Final Account of Life, Corruption, and Death in Putin's Russia*. New York: Random House, 2009.

Sojourner Truth. *This Far by Faith*. See http://www.pbs.org/thisfarbyfaith/people/sojourner_truth.html.

The Voice of Hope: Aung San Suu Kyi: Conversations with Alan Clements. New York: Seven Stories Press, 1997.

Everett Wilson. Review of *Perfect Hostage: A Life of Aung San Suu Kyi, Burma's Prisoner of Conscience*, by Justin Wintle. *Turning Wheel*, Spring 2008, p. 42.

Chapter 9

Women and the Double-edged Sword: Words

All sorrows can be borne if you tell a story about them.

Karen Blixen

In a sense, the world is made of words and stories. In Genesis, the Holy One creates by word of mouth: "And God said . . . ," and it was — the word brought forth the reality it spoke aloud. In a workshop I once asked the question "Are we just the Holy One's stories?" If so, what are we saying? In the Jewish community, it is said that when God, blessed be His Name, spoke at Sinai, the words entered the world, and every Jew can hear these words thousands and thousands of years later. Three of the major religious groups of the world refer to themselves as "The People of the Book." The Christian text of the Gospel of John begins, "In the beginning was the Word, and the Word was with God; and the Word was God; . . . and the Word became flesh and made his dwelling among us" (John 1:1, 14). The mystery of the Incarnation is that God the Word became flesh so that we in our flesh and blood can become words of God — hopefully the good news to the poor, the good news of the fullness of life for all, the good news that we are one with God. Many of our prayers begin, "Speak, Lord, for your servant is listening." In the Orthodox community, the exhortation "Wisdom! Be attentive!" is pronounced three times to the people before any of the readings. In Latin, the word *listen* means "obey." Even in the liturgy of

155

the Eucharist, the last words that each of us speaks before we go to receive the bread and wine, the Body and Blood of Christ as communion with all, are these: "O Lord, I am not worthy to receive you — only say the Word and I shall be healed." We speak the Word; we eat our words; we eat the bread and become what we eat — and go forth as the Word of hope, justice, and peace for all in the world.

This power of the word extends throughout society. There is a custom among the Australian aborigines that when the crop is not growing well and the rice refuses to keep pace with the season and the rain, the women go into the fields. They scatter, then squat down and tell the rice to grow. They tell the rice where it came from and why it is so important to the people — because the rice needs to remember why it is here, why it was created. And they say that the rice grows like nothing you've ever seen after that!

A contemporary writer, Isabel Allende, wrote a book titled *Paula*, dedicated to her only daughter, who was in a long coma in a hospital in Spain. Allende read the story out loud to her. It was medicine for Paula, and Allende hoped against hope that it would both bring her daughter back to consciousness and give her something to fill all the lost hours and days. This is what she told her:

> You have been sleeping for a month now. I don't know how to reach you; I call and call but your name is lost in the nooks and crannies of this hospital. My soul is choked in sand. Sadness is a sterile desert. I don't know how to pray. I cannot string together two thoughts, much less immerse myself in creating a new book. I plunge into these pages in an irrational attempt to overcome my terror. I think perhaps if I give form to this devastation, I shall be able to help you, and myself, and that the meticulous exercise of writing can be our salvation. Eleven years ago I wrote a letter to my grandfather to say goodbye to him in death. On this January 8, 1992, I am writing you, Paula, to bring you back to life.[1]

Words are our lifelines in every situation in which we find ourselves. In Iran and Iraq, they tell the story of Scheherazade. She told the king stories every night, making sure that he did not get bored or drift — it would mean her death. They say it was fear of dying that taught her the art of narration, and each word she spoke was part of the rope that drew her into the next morning and eventually brought the king back to actually living instead of looking only to kill another, since so much of him was already deadened.

The power of the word is almost tangible when spoken aloud. Many who teach English as a second language and anyone who has ever taught an adult to read and write speak of the awe and reverence that the students exhibit when they can actually read and then write their own names — it is as though they are speaking their essence, hearing it in their own ears, and having it sounded out loud for the first time. It gives them a sense of themselves as persons that they were not aware of having before, another level of consciousness that enables them to relate to others more profoundly, more intimately, even more truthfully. In John's Gospel (quoted above), when the Word becomes flesh, others can "see his glory, the glory of the Father's only Son, full of grace and truth." In a sense, it is this grace and truth that become tangible when flesh is translated and articulated into words and names.

Until just recently, this power was experienced often — because certain words and stories were meant to be spoken out loud, not read silently. It is in the hearing that there is meaning, and these sources and levels of power cannot be discovered when one is reading to oneself. This is the oral, spoken, and living word enfleshed in another human being's voice and person. Before there was widespread literacy, reading texts that are considered sacred and are meant to be read in public during rituals was a task reserved for certain people — it was part of their authority and power. But reading aloud also demanded that those entrusted with the task interpreted these texts correctly for all who heard them.

Let's go back to the beginning, because that is where a lot of the "first" stories begin, and a lot of them are lost or hidden in the stories we continue to tell. As the Jewish people read their Scripture, they say it is "black fire on white fire" — the black fire being the type on the pages, and the white fire being the pages, the spaces between the words. They say that there are as many (if not more) stories contained in, embedded in the white fire as there are in the black fire. For instance, after the story of the Holy One creating humans "in their own image, in the divine image — male and female they are created," there seems to be a dearth of females. When Adam and Eve are exiled from the garden, we read that they have children — Cain and Abel, two sons. But obviously they had daughters too; otherwise, how did the human race flourish? It says in Genesis 4 that Cain had relations with his wife, and she conceived and bore Enoch — and then there is the first genealogy, where there are names of the wives included. Sadly enough, in that first genealogy, the only one to speak is Lamech. He is speaking to his wives, Adah and Zillah, and he tells of killing a man and a boy. In the line of Cain, this is what he is remembered for — the only thing. And this is hardly expressive of how God made human beings — in the image of God the creator, the God of life, the God of the living.

The record continues to be primarily of men and their evil deeds. Finally things get so bad that the Holy One decides to destroy creation and everyone on the face of the earth — except Noah and his family. And so we have the story of the ark. But if this was the case — if the wanton disregard for human life was primarily the practice of men in the beginning — why is it that women are blamed for the evil in the world — and theirs (in the Christian tradition) is the "original sin"? The word *sin* is first used in Genesis 4, and not in relation to Eve, but to Cain:

> The LORD looked with favor on Abel and his offering, but on Cain and his offering he did not. Cain greatly resented this and was crestfallen. So the LORD said to Cain: "Why are you so resentful and crestfallen? If you do well, you can hold up your head; but if not, sin is a demon lurking at the door; his urge is toward you, yet you can be his master." (Gen. 4:4b-7)

And Cain's response to God's words, his way of expressing his resentment, is to go out and murder his brother — to commit fratricide. This is the first sin, the original sin. And yet there is so much tradition which says that original sin is Eve eating a piece of fruit and disobeying the command that Yahweh gave to Adam. But Adam must have passed on the information to Eve, since she was not yet created when he was told not to eat of the fruit of the tree of the knowledge of good and bad. What if the interpretation of the tradition just isn't true?

In Genesis 2 and 3 we find the second story of creation — an older one, not necessarily taken from the Jewish traditions, but part of other cultures' stories. It has a great deal to say about agriculture, water, why human beings are farmers, why a man leaves his family of origin to marry a woman of another tribe, and the radical equality of men and women. When Genesis 2 ends, the "earthlings," as they are described — made of the ground, the water, and the breath of God — are of two expressions: a man and a woman. The last line is critical: "The man and his wife were both naked, yet they felt no shame" (Gen. 2:25). They are created beings, with bodies capable of sex and procreation, but without consciousness or awareness, without recognition of the other as a person, without a sense of separateness of identity. They are not yet human beings.

Genesis 3, which is usually looked at as a separate story, is the continuation of the creation of humans — how human beings, men and women, became conscious, became capable of using their free will and choosing, and learning to deal with the consequences of their actions. This chapter also notes all of the other things that human beings have to cope with as a consequence of Adam and Eve's choice: suffering, the pain of childbirth, hard manual labor, lack of control over the weather and the land, and, ultimately, death.

And yet, what does the story really say? Let us listen. The serpent is in the garden, and he approaches the woman. She has heard the command from Adam, but he obviously changed it somewhat, because when the serpent says, "Oh, you can't eat of any of the fruit in the garden," she seeks to correct him, saying, "No — only of the one tree. We are not allowed to even touch it lest we die." However, that is not what God told Adam. This is what God said: "You are free to eat from any of the trees of the garden, except the tree of the knowledge of good and bad. From that tree you shall not eat; the moment you eat from it, you are surely doomed to die" (Gen. 2:16-17). And then the story continues. Listen:

159

The woman saw that the tree was good for food, pleasing to the eyes and desirable for gaining wisdom. So she took some of its fruit and ate it; and she also gave some to her husband, who was with her, and he ate it. Then the eyes of both were opened, and they realized that they were naked; so they sewed fig leaves together and made loincloths for themselves. (Gen. 2:6-7)

So much hangs on the interpretation. First of all, this is all in the plural in Hebrew, so it is told of both Eve and Adam together; this is not a situation in which Eve does any "luring" or "tempting" of Adam. And the woman is discerning: the tree *is* good for food, *is* pleasing to the eye (offering both nutrition and beauty); and it *is* desirable for gaining wisdom! And then she takes some of the fruit from the tree of the *knowledge* of good and bad — notice it is not "evil" or "sinful" — and the consequences are knowledge, consciousness. She and Adam realize that they are naked, and that they are different from each other, and capable of more than just sex and procreation, unlike all else that has been created before them. And they begin their lives as actual human beings, seeking to cover their inner nakedness — their vulnerability, their separateness, their uniqueness, and their private inner lives — as well as their outer nakedness. And they will die, as do all human beings — that is part of being human. To live forever in an Eden, without thought, without choice, without need, and without resourcefulness, creativity, or imagination is not to be human. Now they are conscious and aware that they are made in the image and likeness of the Holy One. The fruit was necessary for the gaining of wisdom — and for many religions, Judaism and Christianity included, the attainment of wisdom is the essence of being human. For Buddhists, it is enlightenment; for others, union with God, communion with all else — in a word, living with wisdom.

What if the original sin is fratricide, and the original story tells us that there are certain rules one must break in order to become more fully human, and that choosing what will lead us to wholeness involves reaching for wisdom, though there are consequences? To be human is to be born, to live, and to die — and to be human religiously is to do this seeking wisdom, seeking God, who is Wisdom Incarnate.

What if Eve — who reflected on whether or not to take the fruit and eat it — decided to do so because of its nutritional value, its beauty, and most especially its wisdom. What if wisdom — actually living consciously like God, with God, and for God — is worth the risk, even the risk of dying? What if part of becoming more human is being willing to risk death on behalf of wisdom — and being able to share that wisdom with others?

Nadine Gordimer, a South African author, puts this succinctly: "Responsibility is what awaits outside the Eden of Creativity." Author Jill Briscoe puts it in a more Christian context: "Jesus' example was radical. Over and over he tried to tell people to differentiate between tradition and truth — and he called them to follow the truth, which abolishes prejudice."[2] And ever since Eve and all those unnamed women in the written histories and religious texts were born into the world, along with men, women have sought to speak, to find their voice and have it heard, to become literate, to speak on behalf of others, and to imaginatively, creatively use words to share their experience, their knowledge of good and bad, their wisdom, and their lives.

Lots of women have, of course, tried and risked their lives repeatedly to speak the truth, to make meaning out of words, and, often, to contradict the prevailing traditions for new wisdom and insights. Let us begin by looking at the words of a few women from history:

Holy Wisdom in your power, hold us fast in every hour.
Enclose us in your threefold wings spreading to embrace
    all things.
One pierces heaven's heights above, another touches earth
    with love.
The other moves with tender care in mystery through the
    cosmic air.
Holy Wisdom in your power, enlighten us in every hour.
                                        Hildegard of Bingen[3]

Christ embodies the ideal of human perfection: in him all bias and defects are removed, and the masculine and feminine virtues are united and their weaknesses redeemed; therefore, his true follow-

161

ers will be progressively exalted over their natural limitations. That is why we see in holy men a womanly tenderness and a truly maternal solicitude for the souls entrusted to them while in holy women there is manly boldness, proficiency, and determination.

Edith Stein[4]

The coming of the Kingdom is perpetual. Again and again, freshness, novelty, power from beyond the world, break in by unexpected paths, bringing unexpected change. Those who cling to tradition and fear all novelty in God's relation with his world deny the creative activity of his Holy Spirit, and forget that what is now tradition was once innovation; that the real Christian is always a revolutionary, belongs to a new race, and has been given a new name and a new song.

Evelyn Underhill[5]

The language, style, and vocabulary may be stilted, or indicative of another historical era, but the thoughts and the meanings still emerge and reveal mystery and truth that often has yet to be acknowledged or absorbed into contemporary spirituality and theology.

Catherine of Siena (1347-1380), one of three Doctors of the Church, was a woman of medieval society who overturned many ideas of what a woman should and should not do. She lived only thirty-three years, but left behind a wealth of letters, essays, prayers, and exhortations to her followers and to public figures. She is one of the patronesses of Europe, along with St. Bridget of Sweden and St. Teresa Benedicta of the Cross. This is the way Catherine was described recently by Timothy Radcliffe, O.P., when he was Master of the Dominicans:

Catherine refused to resign herself in the face of this suffering and division [the Black Death and the decline and split of the church]. In the words of Pope John Paul II, she "dived into the thick of the ecclesiastical and social issues of her time." She addressed political and religious rulers, either in person or through letters, and clearly told them their faults and their Christian duty. She did not hesitate even to tell the Pope that he must be brave and go back to Rome.

She went to the prisons and cared for the poor and the sick. She was consumed by an urgency to bring God's love and mercy to everyone.

Above all, she struggled for peace. She was convinced that "not by the sword or by war or by violence" could good be achieved, but "through peace and through constant humble prayer." Yet she never sacrificed truth or justice for a cheap or easy peace. She reminded the rulers of Bologna that to seek peace without justice was like smearing ointment on a wound that needed to be cauterized. She knew that to be a peacemaker was to follow the steps of Christ, who made peace between God and humanity. And thus the peacemaker must sometimes face Christ's own fate, and suffer rejection. The peacemaker is "another Christ crucified." Our own world is also torn by violence, ethnic and tribal violence in Africa and the Balkans; the threat of nuclear war; violence in our cities and families. Catherine invites us to have the courage to be peacemakers, even if this means that we must suffer persecution and rejection ourselves.[6]

Catherine wanted peace, between cities and nations, within the church, in families, and among her own followers. It was the church that brought forth her strongest language, her most insistent call to conversion, and her blunt exhortation to look at what they were doing, stop, and listen to their own words, and sometimes silences, and see how they were destroying the church, people's faith, and any possibility of preaching the gospel. Again, Radcliffe quotes Catherine and urges not only the Dominicans but all believers to put her words into practice and to live with the same passion that she did:

The Church in our time also suffers from divisions, caused by misunderstanding, intolerance, and loss of "the warmth of charity and peace." Today the love of the Church is often assumed to mean an uncritical silence. One must not "rock the boat"! But Catherine could never be silent. She wrote to some cardinals, "Be silent no longer. Cry out with a hundred thousand voices. I see the world is destroyed through silence. Christ's spouse is pallid, her colour has been drained from her." May St. Catherine teach us her deep love of the Body of Christ, and the wisdom and courage to speak truthfully and openly with words that unite rather than divide, which illuminate rather than obscure, and which heal rather than wound.[7]

Catherine was a woman of her times, yet she used power and authority that came not from those who held authority in the church and society, but from the gifts of the Spirit. She had great respect for the church and believed that one was to be obedient to its leaders, but somehow she also believed that one had a right and a duty to confront the leaders of the church and to criticize them openly and repeatedly in public, in letters and exhortations. She was careful and polite, and yet demanded that they look to their own behaviors, words, and consciences because they were not acting or using their authority as it was given and intended, and they were using it without truth, grace, or the love that Jesus preached. This is what she wrote to the pope:

> My dearest babbo, forgive my presumption in saying what I've said — what I am compelled by gentle First Truth to say. This is his will, father; this is what he is asking of you. . . . Since he has given you authority and you have accepted it, you ought to be using the power and strength that is yours. If you don't intend to use it, it would be better and more to God's honor and the good of your soul to resign. . . .[8]

She would say things like "God is insulted"; "I am exhausted waiting for you to do something"; "others are scandalized"; "God's servants are tormented." She would refer personally in her letters to the leaders, pastors, and administrators within the church as "fragrant flowers" and as "wolves, devils incarnate, and stinking weeds, full of impurity and avarice, and bloated with pride, who poison and corrupt the garden."[9]

To Charles V, the king of France, she wrote about justice and his own part in not doing what was needed — teaching him morality and calling him to public accountability. She reminds him that all his power, authority, wealth, armies, lands, and so on are given to him

164

"on loan," and that a reckoning of what he has done with it will be forthcoming — from God. And then she tells him what to do, and that he'd better do it — or else pay the consequences for his lack of action:

> The second thing I am asking is that you uphold true holy justice. Let it not be adulterated by selfish love for yourself or by flattery or by human respect. And don't pretend not to see if your officials are inflicting injustice for money, denying the poor their rights. . . . No more, for the love of Christ crucified! Don't you realize that you are the cause of this evil if you don't do what you can?[10]

Catherine loved the church and was committed to the truth. She referred to God as First Truth and Jesus as Sweet Truth, and she saw the two as intimately connected to each other. She saw it as "her duty to pressure the Church" with her words, and to pressure God with her prayers and tears of compassion, and to make sure her own and others' tears brought forth compassion for all those in need. She forthrightly taught her followers that the Spirit of God saves us through each other. This is Catherine of Siena through the eyes of Mary Catherine Hilkert in *Speaking with Authority: Catherine of Siena and the Voices of Women Today:*

> Amid plague and wars, poverty and papal politics, hunger for survival and hunger for the Word of God, she heard a call to do what women did not do. She embraced a vocation to preach on hillsides and to the curia, to pray in the classic language of the church and in words that had the authority of only her experience, to share the mission of her brother preachers when women of the word were supposed to be enclosed in monasteries. She initiated a ministry of peacemaking in a world of politics where she had little expertise; she took stands in complex political situations. When she could not see the way forward, she nevertheless voiced words of protest to family and friends, to world and church: this cannot go on. Even as a young woman she gathered friends and disciples and shared with them the unspeakable joy of God's love. Without the appropriate education or titles, she authored letters that changed

165

people's lives and became classics of Italian literature. The theological and mystical classic for which she has been recognized as Doctor of Wisdom reflects the riches of the tradition, but also adds new insights to that same tradition. The scriptures and the liturgy of the church formed her into both devoted disciple and keen critic.[11]

But this hunger to speak the truth is not only or even primarily found within the church, or coming from the mouths, pens, and writings of theologians and religious women. It is found strong and true, imaginative and engaging, refreshing and startling in writers, poets, musicians, dancers, potters — those who use any art form to speak and express the wisdom of their bodies, minds, and souls.

One remarkable poet is Denise Levertov (1923-1997), who came from England to America — New York — in 1947. She considered herself half-Celt and half-Jew: her mother was Welsh, and her father was a Russian Jew of the Hasidim who converted to Christianity as an Anglican priest and a scholar of Jewish mysticism. She herself claimed to honor and celebrate mystery everywhere.

She was in love with the world, but torn by it — world wars, nuclear weapons, nationalism, then the Vietnam war, the death of her sister and friends, the cry in the streets of the sixties, and the fluctuating politics of her times. She was the poetry editor of *The Nation* magazine and a part-time teacher, and she protested with her words and in protest marches and visits to Hanoi and Moscow. She divorced in 1973, over differences of understanding how what was happening in the world and in her writing impacted her private life. She would say in interviews that writing a poem was "summoning the divine" and that it wasn't all that different from what people did in a temple or a church.

Levertov became a Christian when she was writing the long poem "Mass for the Day of St. Thomas Didymus" around 1979. But she kept exploring various traditions, searching for depth and connection. Some say that it was her friends — Dorothy Day; Dan Berrigan; Thomas Merton; Archbishop Raymond Hunthauson of Seattle, Washington; Bishop Thomas Gumbleton of Detroit, Michigan; Brother David Steindl-Rast; Franciscan Murray Bodo; and Dom Helder Camara of

Recife, Brazil — who drew her eventually into the Catholic Church through their writings, their witness to justice and peace, and their care for the poor. When Levertov was baptized in 1988, she told her godmother that she wasn't devoted to the structures or the dogmas or a lot of the people who were leaders, but she was drawn deeply into the Gospels, the traditions of mysticism, and the struggle to speak truthfully about moral issues, and that now that she was in the church, she would be a loyal critic and speak the truth in her way to those who were now her own.

There is a poem by Levertov that is passed around among those who struggle for justice and peace, those who flag in their dedication and then, encouraged by another, stand up again, speak out again. In the words of this poem, called "Beginners," these people find companionship for the journey of faith and the healing of the world. Here are the first few lines:

> But we have only just begun to love the earth.
> We have only begun to imagine the fullness of life.
> How could we tire of hope? — so much is in bud. . . .

Another remarkable woman is Terry Tempest Williams, a sixth-generation Mormon from Salt Lake City, Utah. She and her family laid pipe and put in natural gas lines, water lines, sewage lines, and optic-fiber cables across the West. Now she lives on the edge of America's Red Rock Wilderness in southern Utah. She speaks of the paradox of growing up on the land and making a living from it — in a sense contributing to its destruction and yet loving every bit of its space and openness. She speaks of its power:

> For me, it always come back to the land, respecting the land, the wildlife, the plants, the rivers, mountains and deserts, the absolute essential bedrock of our lives. This is the source of where my power lies, the source of where all our power lies. We are animal. We are Earth. We are water. We are a community of human beings living on this planet together. We forget that. We become disconnected, we lose our center point of gravity, that stillness that allows us to

listen to life on a deeper level and to meet each other in a fully authentic and present way.[12]

Terry Tempest Williams speaks plainly, lyrically, of earth, politics, and economics, of writing and words. She has had speaking engagements cancelled because she has been labeled as "dangerous to students, threatening to the university." One university "uninvited" her because of past comments she had made and because she refused to sign a contract that demanded that she "would not represent a particular point of view and that she would not publicly criticize the President of the United States." But the students organized and invited her on their own, enraged that their rights to freedom of speech were being denied by their university. She had recently written the book *The Open Space of Democracy,* and she was pleased that the students not only had read it but had committed civil disobedience and, in that way, had practiced it.

Williams uses her writing to speak about justice and what is closest to her heart — the land, the earth, and all that dwell on it. When she was arrested for crossing the line at the Nevada Test Site in the Mojave Desert, the arresting officer searched her body and found a notebook and pen in her boots. When asked what they were, she replied, "Weapons." Surprisingly, the officer tucked them back in her boots! She says,

> Writing can be a powerful tool toward justice. Story bypasses rhetoric and pierces the heart. We feel it. Stories have the power to create social change and inspire community. But good writing must stay open to the questions and not fall prey to the pull of a polemic; otherwise, words simply become predictable, sentimental, and stale.[13]

For Williams, the bonds between her writing, her personal life, her politics, and the environment are all of one skein. They cannot be separated. When asked why she did civil disobedience in regard to nuclear testing, she was crystal clear about how she perceives what she does and what she writes, and how it all affects us personally:

. . . I think direct political action, civil disobedience, in particular, is something to be taken very seriously. I belong to "a clan of one-breasted women," where nine women in my family have all had mastectomies; seven have died as a result of nuclear testing and radioactive fallout. We are downwinders. As we speak, my brother is in the last stages of lymphoma. There are times we have to put our body on the line for what we believe, for the injustices we see even within our own families.[14]

Nowdays Williams divides her time between three places: Salt Lake City, Utah, where she is the Annie Clark Taylor Scholar in Environmental Humanities at the University of Utah; Wilson, Wyoming; and Castle Valley, Utah, where she is the "Eminent Writer-in-Residence," the first to fill the post. She works online, with students and residents around the state, dealing with economic issues, oil-and-gas boom and bust, the reservations, and development. She has drawn students of creative writing into the political sphere, asking them to deal with what it means to use their tools, their gifts, their words to illuminate the issues that are impacting the lives of all around them: How can they be of use, of service? What is the role of the writer as witness?

Her concerns are many, and complex: a sense of place, stories, family, others' stories, refuge in the face of despair, loss, death, disease, being part of the clan of the "one-breasted women," dying because of closeness to the place they love and are rooted in, her love of the desert. She says she believes in a "God beyond God." Because of her public readings, her writing, and her speaking, she is hassled by the IRS, hassled on planes and in security areas. After a great deal of public engagement, she decided that this part of her life was snuffing out her poetry, her essays, and her ability to speak of the land, to draw sustenance from community. This is how she explained it to an interviewer in *Image* magazine: "On September 10, 2002, I was in Maine on vacation, and I realized that in this year of speaking publicly, my rhetoric had become as brittle as that of those I was opposing. I had lost my poetry. I went down to the shore — it was just after dusk — and I said prayers. I stood before the rising tide and said to the sea, *Give me one wild word that I can follow.*"[15]

Her book titles tell a story of her journey, her interwoven lives, her questions, and to some extent, where she finds enough answers to hope, to grow, to write again, to keep on. Some of these titles are *Refuge: An Unnatural History of Family and Place; An Unspoken Hunger: Stories from the Field; Desert Quartet: An Erotic Landscape; Leap; Red: Passion and Patience in the Desert; The Open Space of Democracy;* and *Finding Beauty in a Broken World.*

In 2002, Williams went to Rwanda, and it marked her profoundly. It changed the structure of her family when she and her husband, Brooke, adopted a Rwandan boy. In her latest book, *Finding Beauty in a Broken World,* she speaks of one word — *mosaic* — which was going to be the title of the book. Instead, it led her to working with Rwandan women and asking questions about "how to create peace by hand." She speaks of African writer Nadine Gordimer's challenge to find out what is the "essential gesture" right now. At the end of her interview in *Image,* she tells the story, short and provoking, that has started her asking her next set of questions — for her life, her writing, her communities, her politics, her spirituality. She explains that she was interviewed by a young Rwandan woman named Clementine:

> She had two questions for me: "What do you cultivate, and how many children do you have?" I had to say: "I don't cultivate anything. The food I eat, I buy. And I don't have any children." I remember how puzzled she was. She looked at me and said: "Then I have no further questions." I realized in that moment [that] metaphors are not enough. I may cultivate ideas, but what about the cultivation of food? Can I redirect my priorities? And if I do, what might the outcome be, physically and spiritually? And what has been the source of my own birthing process? My books? These are humbling questions. In the brokenness, the distractedness of our lives, we see a poverty of another kind. Even in that war-torn country, there was a wholeness and integrity that was tied to the land through the women.
>
> And yet they are undergoing a transformation also, asking tough questions of their own. With a majority of women in parliament, the Rwandan government is now saying, "We must think about family planning." This has been hugely controversial. Some

women are saying, "If you have us engage in family planning, that's another form of genocide." But a younger generation is saying, "We must consider what the land can sustain." The roots of genocide are complex, not only tied to colonialism and racial preference — Tutsi versus Hutu — but also a poverty tied to the land, tied to density issues, deforestation and erosion.

These questions become the concerns of us all, local and global dilemmas that ask us to engage creatively, constructively, and to employ a depth of listening we may not have known before, one that cultivates authentic relationships that inevitably give birth to meaningful actions.[16]

Perhaps a good way to end this section on this woman and her dreams and writings is to quote a paragraph from one of her books, *Leap,* which is a long discussion of/reflection on a painting by Hieronymus Bosch called *The Garden of Earthly Delights*. It is a densely packed painting, complex, crowded with individuals, small pieces that are groups of people who tell stories, animals, birds, food, layers upon layers of living, dying, suffering, rejoicing, dancing, writhing in pain, working — a universe in itself. When Williams looks at the painting, it evokes her memories — of family, Mormonism, theology, her personal choices, her personal life, her landscapes, her priorities. She is always looking for the heart of a painting — its essence, why it was created — and she decides that for Bosch this essence is a wound: it is our separation from God and so from each other and the earth itself. The painting itself is five hundred years old, decaying, now in the process of being restored — resurrected. This is what Williams writes:

Our wound, our separation from the Sacred, the pain of our isolation, may this be the open door that leads us to the table of restoration, may we sit around the table, may we break bread around the table, may we stand on top of the table, may we turn the table over and dance, leap, leap for joy, all this in the gesture of conserving a painting, conserving a landscape, conserving a spirit, our own restored spirits once lost, now found, Paradise found, right here on this beautiful blue planet called Earth.[17]

And the last woman in this chapter is Ivone Gebara, a Brazilian Sister of Notre Dame, a philosopher, a theologian — in fact, one of Latin America's foremost feminist liberation theologians. That's a long list of what she "is," but in reality she listens to women, poor women, women of the Third World, women who most theologians and people in the church and society rarely think about, let alone listen to. Most don't ask their opinions or ask about their experience of life, of suffering and death, of good and evil, of God and the crosses they bear, often laid on them by others and the evil they do themselves. And Gebara reflects on how women are destroyed in so many ways by the theology that others — primarily traditional, male, hierarchical structures — do. She is interested in critique, but more interested in how to do theology that creates solidarity and freedom for all women and men, and seeks to incorporate women's experience and knowledge into the equations and proclamations of religion.

Gebara teaches at the Theology Institute of Recife (ITER) in Brazil, and she spends her time in the barrios and favelas with women and children, the elderly and infirm, the unemployed, those struggling not only to survive in the midst of lack and violence but to live fully as human beings, as women. Her primary books are *Longing for Running Water: Ecofeminism and Liberation; Trinity: A Word on Things New and Old; Mary: Mother of God, Mother of the Poor;* and her latest book, *Out of the Depths: Women's Experience of Evil and Salvation.*

In this last book, Gebara explains what she is about — what has taught her, what has brought her evil, what has freed her, and why she does theology the way she does:

What a contradictory evil! How to bear being a woman theologian and, still more, a theologian of liberation? What a bizarre suffering! My trouble as a theologian began with a certain independence of thought. Independent research, looked upon as a good, has brought evil to me. As long as I echoed the ideas of others, there was no conflict. I could serve as a professor of theology and philosophy; that is, I could prepare my courses, using books of theology and philosophy written by men, and I never had a problem. I was highly appreciated and considered a competent professor.

But the season for ripe fruit came, and with it the wish and the desire to say my own word. Independence led me to live a considerable distance from my colleagues, mostly men. One reason for maintaining this distance was my attachment to a feminist perspective. Such a perspective was often considered a problem of the First World trying to co-opt us. But my experience of working with different groups of women, especially women at the grass roots, showed me that they had something special to consider, a specific oppression experienced by women.[18]

Gebara goes on to speak of the rise of liberation theology and the questions it posed to the larger church and world. The problems of poverty and oppression, of how evil and human sin touched every aspect of existence, were not to be viewed as one issue of theology among many others; they were to be seen as core to all the issues. Somehow, the issue of liberation — and of women — is at the very heart of both goodness and oppression, injustice, and violence. Gebara expresses this precisely: "Liberation was the substance of all theology; in short, liberation and theology should be correlative terms."[19] And she adds to this position what is essential to what must be examined and taken into account now:

Similarly, I would say that feminism, or the marginalization of women, is not just one more theme but that the appearance of women on the public stage of history had to change the very structure of the theological enterprise, taking this new problematic into account. Given the "explosion of women in the midst of the explosion of the poor," as feminists of the Third World were saying, it is no longer possible to maintain the same trends of thought or to repeat the same theological formulas. Something very deep within the human person was beginning to awaken. And that necessitated a more inclusive theology, one that took account of different experiences of and approaches to the mystery of God, a theology that elaborated Christology in broader and less sexist categories than had existed up to now.[20]

173

In John's Gospel, while Jesus is speaking with his friends and disciples in the portion of the text that is often referred to as "the last discourse," Jesus has something to say that has rarely, if ever, been alluded to or delved into with any kind of research. He says to them that he is leaving and that he will send the Advocate, the Spirit of Truth, to them. Earlier he has told them that the Spirit will remind them of everything that he has spoken and taught. Now he tells them the Spirit of Truth has another work and gift too:

> I have much more to tell you, but you cannot bear it now. But when he comes, the Spirit of truth, he will guide you to all truth. He will not speak on his own, but he will speak what he hears, and will declare to you the things that are coming. He will glorify me, because he will take from what is mine and declare it to you. Everything that the Father has is mine; for this reason I told you that he will take from what is mine and declare it to you. (John 16:12-15)

Those words are fraught with power, with expectation, with anticipation and possibility. "I have much more to tell you, but you cannot bear it now." Perhaps we can bear it now — in fact, perhaps we are in desperate need of what the Spirit of Truth wishes to share with us and declare to us now, in this new millennium. The nature of the Spirit is constant transformation, ever the same and ever new — so new that it could not be imagined before, and there was no vocabulary or words to express it. But the Spirit of Truth takes from Jesus and all that the Father has given to Jesus and passes it on — to whomever the Spirit wishes — blowing the breath of truth wherever the Spirit wills. The Spirit is speaking. Are we listening?

I hope that this chapter begins to open up the possibilities of lists, litanies of women you will remember: theologians, writers, poets, preachers, potters, dancers, musicians, philosophers, activists, environmentalists — all midwives to the Truth and its limitless expressions. I left so many out: Monika Hellwig, Elsa Tamez, Sister Wendy Beckett, Juana Ines de la Cruz, Phyllis Trible, Chung Hyun Kyung, Rebecca Chopp, Sallie McFague, Elisabeth Moltmann-Wendel, Dorothee Soelle, Diana

Hayes, Paula Gunn Allen, Joy Harjo, Barbara Kingsolver, Madeleine L'Engle, Kristen Lavenstadder, Nadine Gordimer, Flannery O'Connor, Emma Lazarus, Susan Sontag, Grace Paley, Julia Esquivel, Hannah Arendt, Simone Weil, Hildegard Goss-Mayr, Franziska Jagerstatter, Mairead Maguire, Helen Prejean, Jean Donovan, Dorothy Kazel, Ita Ford, Maura Clark, Jane Addams, Karen Silkwood, Helen Caldicott, Viola Liuzzo, Catherine de Vinck, Catherine de Hueck Doherty, Eileen Egan, Elizabeth McAlister, Marie Dennis, Joan Baez, along with all the other singers: Marian Anderson, Nina Simone, Violeta Parra. . . .

You must have your own litany of remembrance. These are all the people you're waiting to meet with in the kingdom of justice and peace, sit at table with and talk, sing, laugh, and cry about it all. My list is really so long — I've been keeping it since I was about fourteen — that I think I will need until forever just to start getting to know these women.

Sources Used in This Chapter

Colleen Carpenter Cullinan. "Red Is the Colour of the Morning: Resurrection in the Writing of Terry Tempest Williams." *The Way* 48, no. 2 (April 2009): 25-39.

Ivone Gebara. *Out of the Depths: Women's Experience of Evil and Salvation.* Trans. Ann Patrick Ware. Minneapolis: Augsburg Fortress Press, 2002.

Dana Greene. "Denise Levertov: A Poet's Pilgrimage." *National Catholic Reporter,* Opinion and Arts, 27 April 2007, pp. 14-15.

Heidi Hart. "A Conversation with Terry Tempest Williams." *Image: Art, Faith, Mystery,* issue 58, pp. 59-72.

Mary Catherine Hilkert. *Speaking with Authority: Catherine of Siena and the Voices of Women Today.* Mahwah, N.J.: Paulist Press, 2008.

The Letters of Catherine of Siena. 2 volumes. Translated by Suzanne Noffke. Tempe, Ariz.: Arizona Center for Medieval and Renaissance Texts and Studies, 2000-2001.

Timothy Radcliffe, O.P. "St. Catherine of Siena (1347-1380), Patroness of Europe: A Letter to the Dominican Order, Published April 2000, to Celebrate the Naming of St. Catherine of Siena as One of the Patrons of Europe." Find this at http://www.op.org/international/english/Documents/masters_order/Radcliffe/catherine_s 2/5/2006.

Barbara Reid, O.P. *Taking Up the Cross: New Testament Interpretations through Latina and Feminist Eyes.* Minneapolis: Fortress Press, 2007.

"Terry Tempest Williams," interview in *The Progressive* with David Kupfer, February 2005, pp. 35-40.

Chapter 10

And You — and Us —
What Will Be Remembered of Us?

And what do you plan on doing with your one wild and precious life?

Mary Oliver, "The Summer Day"

I remember the first time I visited the Taj Mahal in Agra, India. We had come from Delhi on a train, then a bus, then a taxi. Then we walked the back streets of the markets and in under a stone doorway. As we came in and walked down the long avenue, the Taj was at the end, shining in the sunlight. Its beauty was stunning, and we just stood there and tried to absorb it, to soak it in. There is a huge reflecting pool in front of it, and the double image is disorienting at first. Which image is the actual building?

We spent the entire day and evening there to see how the Taj changed and shimmered and moved in varying degrees of sunlight, shadow, shade, and finally nightfall to pitch darkness. Even the moon accommodated us and rose, shedding its light on the Taj's whiteness. There was so much to take in. Up close, the mosaics were intricate and detailed in color and placement. Each small stone or jewel was hand-picked, glued into part of a pattern — a flower, a spiraling star, an eye. I'd have to step back to see that that small pattern was part of a larger pattern — a bush, or a branch, or a bird — and then step back again to see a larger pattern yet: a whole tree laced into one slab of marble, one piece in a side wall. And then I was filled with amazement yet again when I realized that the wall I was looking at mirrored another wall on the other side of the building or was part of a pattern of eight walls.

As I would look at each tiny fragment, another visitor, usually an Indian woman who had been there often, would tell me that behind the image you could see yet another image that was hidden inside the first, unnoticed unless it was pointed out to you! And then she would smile and ask, "Are you staying all day and into the night? You must see it at this time of day — and in the reflecting pool too — morning freshness, blinding light and heat of noon, shadows lengthening, pitch blackness, and moonlight." Everyone wanted their picture taken to see what they looked like against it, as backdrop to their life. The women would wear or carry their brightest scarves and saris to stand out in color against the cold marble.

Then I read the story of how the Taj Mahal was built — by slave labor, causing the deaths of thousands of people. If the laborer's work satisfied the overseer, he would live and be fed, and perhaps his family would reap some daily benefits. If the laborer's work did not satisfy the overseer, he could lose a hand, a finger, an eye, or even his life. The Taj was built by the king to honor his favorite wife, who had died in childbirth. The building of this magnificent structure used brutality in order to produce beauty; it involved oppression, starvation, and violence so that one with power could proclaim his love and, of course, show his own power and glory. Ironically, this king ended up imprisoned by his son across the river. His cell had a small window looking out at the magnificence of the building he had created to his own memory and the woman he loved.

As we left, we were given pamphlets describing the slow erosion and destruction of the Taj. Pollution in the air and water are causing damage. Cracks and discoloration in the marble are forming. In many places, small pieces of stone or jewels are falling out of the glue or being picked out deliberately. Time and wear and tear are taking their toll on this piece of architecture, as on all things.

As I was going back on the train, I reflected on the interlacing, the complexities, and the minute pieces needed to form this immense structure. I thought about the long labor, the pain and suffering, and even the violence that had created such glorious loveliness, beauty that was reflected back in the water and that could be so different in varying weather, times, and seasons. But what struck me most was how there was such diversity in the structure, and yet it was all of a piece, with a oneness that depended on vast differences — and how much it was made of sorrow. And I realized that this is a remarkable symbol for women's theology and spirituality. It is emblematic of how women do theology in a world that is harsh and demanding. The formation of women's theology, like the building of the Taj, can often be done as a paean to love or to a woman or to a god. Yet it is made of blood, bones, torn flesh, death as much as life, pain and slavery, misused authority and power. Yet, despite this suffering, something remains for generations after that speaks truth to others, that asks immortal questions. Even stone sings with hope in what has been or can still be in the world.

This book has looked at women, individuals, their families and friends. It has looked at the myriad ways of living and so of doing theology and expressing spirit and belief in the Holy. And a number of priorities of women's theology have emerged, both from the stories of Scripture and from the stories of women from around the world. As a place to begin, this list of the priorities might be helpful:

1. Relieve suffering.
2. Stand witness against the taking of life or harming others, all others, including creation: water, air, land, animals, birds — everything that exists. Prepare all for decent burial, even criminals. Work against extinction; protect what is endangered.
3. Name evil, at its roots and sources, pointing out its effects on people.
4. Change and organize for change with no violence, beginning with resistance based on living, living in solidarity with victims.
5. Endeavor to get children born and, even more so, to keep the children and women healthy.
6. Ensure health care and dignity for all.
7. Make sure there is fresh water, air, food, shelter, and space — the basic necessities of survival — for all.
8. Promote education.

9. Engage in economics to invest in people. Use one's resources and material goods to serve the needs of all — to bring the kingdom of justice and peace.
10. Take care of specific groups: widows, orphans, the victims of violence and injustice, special needs children and adults, minorities, strangers, refugees.
11. Weep and rail against violence and injustice and unnecessary death.
12. Share beauty, the arts, spirituality, wisdom, story, music, medicine, ways of dancing on the earth — the gifts that make life more than mere survival.
13. And do all of this with others, across boundaries, borders, differences of religion, nation, gender, language, culture, and geography.

These priorities are not listed in any order — except perhaps for the first one: *relieve suffering.* In a sense there are three kinds of suffering, gleaned from stories women tell. First, there is suffering that is the normal, usual effect of being human — diminishment of capacities, limitations of possibilities, aging, sickness, accidents, and eventually death. Second, there is suffering that others cause, perpetuate, lay on others, condemn others to, and make profit from. These forms of suffering are violent and destroy the human body, mind, heart, and spirit. They are the effects of injustice, sin, evil executed by choice, systems, and institutional decisions and practice — they can be individual, structural, and/or systemic. Sadly, this is the kind of suffering most often experienced by many in the world — and especially women, children, and the poor. And third, there is suffering that is borne for and with others — picking up another's cross and carrying it for that person to give him or her a rest, or bearing a burden with others, standing in solidarity and communion with them.

But it all comes down to this: What can I do? What can we do? Where do we start? How can we sustain resistance and alternatives that are imaginative, creative, and life-giving? In a sense, this chapter is about ordinary people — not well-known on the national or the international scene, or even within one's religious group. But they are known — to those they serve, those they stand with, those they bring hope to, those they help to find their voice, those who know them as friend or mentor or sister in the struggle to live with respect, dignity, and full humanness. We find them in our families; in the places where we dwell, work, teach, attend school, go to church, work on projects; in our communities and organizations; in our daily lives when we bump into strangers and people we barely know. Our world is full of them.

There is an incredibly short story in the beginning of Mark's Gospel that tells of one such woman. She has no name, but many of us will be anonymous except to those who will remember us because of what we did for them and what we allowed them to do for us. Jesus has "appeared" in Galilee and has begun to preach, travel the roads, and collect followers to his way of life. He goes with the first four disciples he's called after him — Andrew and his brother Simon, and James and his younger brother John — and they go into the synagogue on a Sabbath in Capernaum. This story unfolds as they leave the synagogue and head home for the Sabbath afternoon/main meal:

> On leaving the synagogue he [immediately] entered the house of Simon and Andrew with James and John. Simon's mother-in-law lay sick with a fever. They immediately told him about her. He [immediately] approached, grasped her hand, and helped [raised] her up. Then the fever [immediately] left her and she [immediately] waited on them. (Mark 1:29-31)

It's a familiar story, and yet often we don't actually hear it. In the original, the word *immediately* is used six times, revealing the urgency of Mark's Gospel — everything will happen almost too quickly. The moment "now" must be seized. One action leads immediately into the next, like a stone skipping across water, or a snowball rolling downhill. Once set in motion, it is nearly impossible to stop what will be the consequences. Jesus and the four new followers leave the synagogue, and immediately they go home, to Simon Peter and Andrew's house. This is usually where we go after synagogue or church, after a time of worship — we go home together, or we go back to those who didn't come. When they arrive, Jesus is told immediately that Simon

181

Peter's mother-in-law is sick in bed with a fever. When we leave the place of worship, who are we concerned about immediately? Who is our first responsibility? In this case, it is someone who is sick — and in those days to be ill with a fever, and in bed, was a serious thing. This is a dangerous illness, life-threatening.

And Jesus responds immediately and surprisingly. He goes to her, grasps her by the hand, and raises her up. This is not a comforting, gentle, or soothing touch. It is a strong grasp, and she is pulled to her feet. The word that is used is the word for resurrection — she is raised up, as Jesus will be raised from the dead! He approaches her — as the women will later approach Jesus, with great respect, to honor him. And we are told that the fever immediately leaves her, departs.

In writing this Gospel, Mark knows his community of believers, and he is inspired to use specific words and phrases that they would be familiar with as Jews immersed in the words of the prophets and the traditions of the past. In this first chapter, both here and in the earlier baptismal story at the very beginning of the chapter, he uses Isaiah 42, which speaks of the servant of the Lord, who has been given the Spirit of the Lord — to bring justice to the nations, with no violence, being careful of even a bruised reed and a smoldering wick. This servant of the Lord will be a teacher of justice to all the ends of the earth. Not only does he live in obedience to the creator of all, the one who sustains and keeps us alive, but he will do amazing things. Listen to what he will do!

> I, the LORD, have called you for the victory of justice,
> I have grasped you by the hand;
> I formed you, and set you as a covenant of the people,
> a light for the nations,
> to open the eyes of the blind,
> to bring out prisoners from confinement;
> and from the dungeon, those who live in darkness.
> . . . See, the earlier things have come to pass, new ones,
>   I now foretell;
> before they spring into being, I announce them to you.
>
> (Isa. 42:6-7, 9)

Jesus grasps Simon Peter's mother-in-law by the hand. She is claimed for the victory of justice. She is wrenched away from the powers of darkness and freed from what confines and imprisons her. This is a new thing — she is raised up to be a servant with him, to be part of this new covenant, this light to the nations, bringing justice to all, through compassion and mercy, fierce tenderness and touch. And she "springs up"! Then we are told simply that "she [immediately] waited on them." This last line can often cause groans and moans. Of course — what else would be expected? But in reality she has received power from Jesus, and this power is a new thing. The word used for "wait on them" is the word used in the early church and later in the Gospels to designate the authority and practice of the deacon — the one who would proclaim the gospel in the liturgical assembly, wait on the table, care for the altar, prepare the gifts, share them with the community, and be "the good news" of the Lord in the world, sent out by the community in their name. The deacons and deaconesses would prepare the initiates for baptism and serve as teachers, catechists, and preachers. Simon Peter's mother-in-law rises, begins to wait on them, and becomes not only Jesus' fifth disciple, the first woman disciple, but even more — she becomes the first deaconess! She is just an ordinary woman — Simon Peter's mother-in-law, the mother of his wife — but she is a woman who, in her own right, will be the head of the house church in Capernaum, which will become Jesus' home when he is not on the road.

Which brings us to Simon Peter's wife — her daughter. Where is she? The understanding is that if you're not mentioned by name in the Scriptures, it means that either you're not a follower or you're dead. Far too many women died in childbirth, then as now, and it is thought that Simon Peter's wife may have died that way. Simon Peter would have been perhaps thirty years old. With Andrew he runs the family's fishing business, and he has his own boat. Simon Peter's mother-in-law lives with him, perhaps to take care of his child/children. Some writings mention Petra, a young woman whom many believe to be Simon Peter's daughter. This is family, coping with death, marrying and bearing children, living in occupied territory that is always shadowed by the violent presence of the Roman soldiers and the threat of slow starvation. People take each other in, living as extended family to survive. Simon Peter's mother-in-law becomes a disciple, a deaconess, and the head of the house church out of gratitude for Jesus' presence, his good news of hope, liberation, freedom, and compassion toward her. This new thing of God in Jesus has made her a new thing, too. Do you not see it?

What can one person do? It seems one person can do an enormous amount, once she begins. Simon Peter's mother-in-law uses her house, which she shares with Simon Peter and Andrew and others, as a meeting place for all those in need — crowds of them who "immediately" find themselves at her door, seeking the same compassion, touch, freedom, hope, and wisdom that she now knows in Jesus. We do not hear anything else about her. The story moves on, along with Jesus and his disciples, toward Jerusalem and death. But Jesus and his followers keep coming back to Capernaum until that last trip to the temple and Jesus' death outside the city. What can one person do? She can be the hub, the center ground, the meeting place for those in need, those seeking and searching, those who have gotten wind of good news and have come to check it out. What can one person do? She can live in gratitude, sharing it all, because the richness is never-ending and grows as it is passed on to others.

There is a wonderful children's story from Tibet. When it was told to me, the storyteller simply called it "Rags."

Once upon a time, there was a queen of a great nation. Some of her attendants told her about the stories and teachings of a wise one in the city. She invited the wise one to the palace, and as she listened to the wise one, her spirits were lifted. She began to see that there could be meaning in her life, beyond simply being the wife of the king, a figure who stood by his side and looked beautiful, who came when summoned. She was utterly grateful to the wise one for the teaching and insights, and she sent the wise one a rather large donation of gold. Eventually the king heard about it and was furious. His wife (he thought) was gullible and had probably been taken in and then pressed for the gold. So he summoned this "wise one" to account for the gold.

When the wise one came (the storyteller never said if it was a man or a woman, so let's say that, surprisingly, the wise one was a woman), she told the king the story of what happened to the money and where it went. First, she said, the money was taken to the marketplace (the local economy). Many bolts of new cloth were bought, and all her followers and friends made new suits of clothes for the poor and the beggars of the city. In exchange, the poor gave all their old rags back to the wise one's followers. The rags were washed and made into quilts, and the quilts were distributed to those in need. The old quilts were collected and made into rugs. The old rugs were collected and made into doormats. The old doormats were collected and made into brooms. The old brooms were collected and made into straw. All the old straw was collected and made into bricks. And together the wise one's followers and those who had shared some of the new things gathered and built houses to provide shelter for others, so that many could live in dignity.

And the wise one looked at the king and said, "It is all because of one woman, the queen, who is not naïve at all. Your wife's generosity has set in motion work for justice and the possibility of peace for many in the kingdom. Your good wife has learned that all is given to us as gift, that everything in the universe is entrusted to us to use for and with others and for the care of the earth. We must all learn this and keep remembering it — gifts are meant to be shared. And you," she said, fixing her gaze on the king, "what are you going to do? How generous are you going to be? What have you learned from your wife? What are you going to set in motion now that you have heard the story?"

We began this book with the story of the unnamed woman who anointed the head of Jesus, preparing him for his burial, and who heard him proclaim that she would be remembered forever, wherever the good news is preached in all the world. This woman, who aligned herself with Jesus and publicly sought to ease and comfort him with her solidarity and sharing of a gift and a touch, was more than his disciple. She was his friend. And he was grateful. We learned that perhaps she is not unnamed or unknown, that her name might be Salome, one of the three women named in Mark's Gospel (even more women are mentioned in the other accounts) as the first witnesses to the resurrection

185

— this new thing that has burst into the world, altering history and our lives forever. Perhaps we should look at that last story of Mark's Gospel more closely so that we can learn how to witness to the resurrection — not just as individual women but as women banded together:

> When the sabbath was over, Mary Magdalene, Mary, the mother of James, and Salome bought spices so that they might go and anoint him. Very early when the sun had risen, on the first day of the week, they came to the tomb. They were saying to one another, "Who will roll back the stone for us from the entrance to the tomb?" When they looked up, they saw that the stone had been rolled back; it was very large. On entering the tomb they saw a young man sitting on the right side, clothed in a white robe, and they were utterly amazed [afraid]. He said to them, "Do not be amazed [afraid]! You seek Jesus of Nazareth, the crucified. He has been raised; he is not here. Behold, the place where they laid him. But go and tell his disciples and Peter, 'He is going before you to Galilee; there you will see him, as he told you.'" Then they went out and fled from the tomb, seized with trembling and bewilderment. They said nothing to anyone, for they were afraid. (Mark 16:1-8)

This is the original ending of Mark's Gospel. The rest was added on at various times, because so many had trouble with this abrupt and shocking end. What — the women said nothing to anyone? Then how did we ever come to believe?

Our attention is immediately drawn to the climate of fear. The women live in occupied territory, and the tomb has been sealed. In the older translations, the stone that seals the tomb is described three times as huge. The women are going after the Sabbath is over, in obedience to the law (on the Sabbath, which belonged to God alone, no work could be done), to do a corporal work of mercy, the highest in the Jewish community: preparing a condemned and executed criminal's body for burial — especially one crucified who was considered abandoned by God. They are attempting to do the impossible; they won't even be able to move the stone to get in to the body. In their grief, they go anyway, and that's what they talk about — rather than their loss and their fear. And when they arrive, they find the stone pushed aside.

They enter in fear and see some sort of vision: a young man dressed in white (not the symbol of death, but of life — a baptismal garment of one who comes to preach good news!). The young man's message begins, *"Do not be afraid!"* He knows who they are looking for — Jesus of Nazareth, the crucified one. And his news is startling and even terrifying: Jesus is alive! He's not dead! He's out there, in Galilee, which is home for all of them, and he's waiting for them. Go! Go and tell the rest of the disciples — for the women are his disciples too. Tell Simon Peter, who, because of his betrayal, is on the fringe of the group and so is mentioned separately. Go and tell them that Jesus is waiting for them. And the women's response is one of terror and bewilderment. They bolt and run from the tomb, and in their fear they say nothing to anyone.

"Nothing to anyone" is the crucial phrase. Who is "anyone"? Anyone other than the other disciples and those who came up to Jerusalem for the feast with him? Anyone other than those who had known him, had been touched by him, had been freed from despair by him? Anyone other than those in solidarity with them and who would want to know? They obey. They tell their friends and Jesus' friends. And they go home; they go back to Galilee, where he is waiting for them. It's about ninety miles from Jerusalem to Nazareth, a journey of about ten days to two weeks. It's rough country. They are a group of about 100 to 120 people, of all ages and all walks of life, and they are both grieving and hoping against hope. All the way home they talk. They talk and walk together and tell stories. They remember. They share all that Jesus did for them. They tell their own stories and listen to others' memories of him. And by the time they get to Galilee, they are a community, a family beyond blood and marriage ties — a family birthed in the death of their beloved Jesus, a family birthed in agony and grieving, and now a family birthed in wild exaltation and hope.

But do they see him in Galilee? Mark's Gospel is written in a circle — a spiraling circle. We are told in the first chapter of Mark that Jesus "came to Galilee proclaiming the gospel of God" (Mark 1:14). A better translation would be this: "And Jesus appeared in Galilee proclaiming the gospel of God." Now, in the longer ending of the Gospel of Mark, Jesus appears in Galilee again. The book is written to be read, then re-read, as Jesus' followers remember their own experiences and others' experiences. They are to read it again and again, with others, putting the pieces together and remembering, putting back together their lives and the world the way it was. By re-reading Mark's Gospel, Jesus' followers seek once again to hear, to believe, to follow, and to become the beloved children of God with Jesus, the servants of God in the world, the ones who bear the Spirit of Truth within them. They are to become the gospel, the good news of God — the truth-tellers, those who are the friends of God, the friends of each other, and the friends of the earth. It is a story to be told so often that you learn it by heart and take it to heart and make it come true. And then, finally, you are the story you tell, and you will be remembered for your piece of what transforms the world, alone and with others.

The story says that it takes at least three women (though it's probably easier with more) to set in motion resurrection, new life, a new world, hope, and the wild possibility of the fullness of humanity becoming like God. Even in an impossible situation — when a huge stone is blocking the entrance and preventing you from enacting the simple ritual gesture of preparing a dead body for burial and putting your grief into your hands and wailing voice — you do it anyway! And the beginning, the steps together, the intent, the unspoken words, the sadness and loss that choke your throat and heart, the doing what has to be done in the face of violence, of unnecessary death, of the callousness of the powerful and the demands of law and tradition — it is enough. It will set in motion something new — a way back home, a way back into life with meaning and insight, a way together to transfigure all pain and evil, a way to be human, to be a woman, to be women, to be grace and a force to be reckoned with in the world, to be a blessing, and to be friends walking with care upon the earth and living life ever more abundantly with all.

Augustine of Hippo said, "Hope has two beautiful daughters. Their names are Anger and Courage: anger at the way things are, and courage to see that they do not remain as they are." In a small Russian Orthodox chapel in the middle of nowhere in Alaska, I saw an icon of the

Woman, the Lady Wisdom, and she had three daughters: Faith, Hope, and Love. God's name is Wisdom. God's name is Truth. And God's name is the Word in flesh — Word spoken, told, lived, and coming true. Woman Wisdom has two identical sisters, Truth and Story — a Trinity. And they each give birth to a daughter: Wisdom gives birth to Compassion/Pity. Her name has two meanings: the first is to see and do something about what you see, because what you see makes you so sick that you want to throw up, and you move to touch, to heal, to ease, to soothe. And the other meaning, just as strong, is that what you see makes you so angry that you go into labor and give birth to something new that can transform and alter reality. (The muscles that make us throw up are the same muscles that are used in birthing a child.) Story gives birth to Memory — memory of the ancestors and wise ones, the elders, the traditions and movements of history. But this memory is not a rigid bond or prison. No, this is memory as the scent of hope, of possibility and promise, of what has not been seen or imagined before. And Truth gives birth to Fierceness, to passion and grace, especially under fire and when life is thwarted, despoiled, desecrated. This fierceness is faithful, and sometimes it is sheer endurance that refuses to give up or die. They are all women to be reckoned with and embraced. And they will be praised by all.

They reveal God, by whatever name you call God, as fully human and in balance and harmony with other names, long in use, but without relationship to the other. Male and female they were created, man and woman together. And not specifically one of each — men and women together. For, at root, God is community, friends — intimate, singular, and yet bound in communion together. And there is room in there for everyone — at the moment, about 6.8 billion people (not counting all those who have gone before and all those yet to come). And as the image and likeness of God, we have hearts that are vast enough, deeper than the universe, to hold them all in gratefulness, in awe, in delight, and in freedom. Catherine of Siena said, "For those who believe, all the way home to heaven is heaven." The kingdom of heaven is made home here and now, everywhere on this planet and in this universe, with all of us. We start here, and we hold each other and everything all together in Truth.

I'll end with a story that I've heard told in the northwestern edge of land called Canada by some and Washington state by others, but also told in Bangladesh and in many other areas of southeast Asia during the monsoons. When I told it in South Africa, my listeners smiled — they knew the story too.

Once upon a time, the world wasn't the way it is now. Now the sky is high — way up there in the blue, unreachable, untouchable. But once it was close, much, much closer than you can imagine. In fact, the clouds were so low that your head was in them all the time. The tops of trees were lost in them, and if you built your house higher than a few feet off the ground, it was lost in them too. In fact, the clouds — full of rain, sleet, snow, sometimes even hail and ice — were always in your hair, always dripping, always soaking through everything.

It had been this way for as long as anyone could remember. And most folk spent their lives bent over to keep their heads somewhat dry, so that you saw only people's feet and their shoes, if they had any. Everyone went about their work bent over, and then they crawled into their beds (mostly on the ground), weary and aching from the day. The sun rarely came out, and when it did, all work stopped and people tried lifting their heads and letting the sunshine touch them. It was, of course, harder on the servants, slaves, workers, farmers, those who dug the ditches for water and harvested the food and carried everything back and forth — always bent over.

One day, a servant girl was just plain tired. Her hair was wet, her clothes were soggy, and she was so weary of it all. She stood up straight, and as she did, she lifted the broom that was in her hands and whacked the cloud above her, and she yelled and cursed and whacked it again, and again, and again in frustration and anger and exhaustion. She'd just had enough. Enough! To her surprise, she noticed that with each whack the cloud had moved a little bit away from her and had risen a bit higher. She stopped. Was it possible? She hit the cloud again, and again — and sure enough, it was moving. She was ecstatic, and wild, and loud, screaming and yelling at the other servants to come and see, and she showed them. They were incredulous at first, but it was true. She had made the cloud in the courtyard rise at least a foot or two. They started whacking at it, too. And they called out to the workers with their hoes, rakes, and shovels to come and see, and help them.

And they all went at it, whacking away. But they got tired quickly. This wasn't going to be easy, and it would take a lot of time. The servant girl called out to them, "We have to get organized, and we all have to do one whack at a time together." And so they did. On the count of three: One, two, three — whack! One, two, three — whack! And on and on they went. Soon they realized that the young servant girl was calling out a cadence, a rhythm that they could follow easily together — "One, two, three — whack!" — swinging, easy, graceful. One, two, three — whack again, move to the left, slide along. In this way they learned something new — they were dancing and singing and working together. The rhythm rose and fell, and others joined them. Even their masters and the wealthy, high in their second-story and third-story houses, suddenly found their homes invaded by these tool-toting servants, whacking away at the clouds, and they were stunned to see that the clouds were rising, ever so slowly, above the courtyard, above the houses. It got harder to reach the clouds, so they climbed the trees and went up the hills and into the mountains, teaching everyone as they went along.

One, two, three — whack. One, two, three — whack. One, two, three — whack. This went on for ages, it seemed. But the next generation learned the story because their sky was higher. And so it has been told: "Look up at the sky. See how high it is above us? And remember that it wasn't always that way. Those who went before us, especially the poor, the servants, and the ones who spent so much of their lives bent over — they were the ones who lifted the sky. Now let's look at each other and let's ask ourselves, If they could push the sky, if they could lift the sky so high, then what are we going to do for the next generation, and the one after that — even to the seventh generation? What are we going to be remembered for?"

Something is very gently, invisibly, silently, pulling at me — a thread or net of threads finer than cobweb and as elastic. I haven't tried the strength of it. No barbed hook pierced and tore me. Was it not long ago this thread began to draw me? Or way back? Was I

born with its knowing about my neck, a bridle? Not fear but a stirring of wonder makes me catch my breath when I feel the tug of it
when I thought it had loosened itself and gone.

Denise Levertov, "The Thread"

"Amen. Amen, I say to you: wherever the gospel is told and proclaimed to all the world, what she has done will be told in memory
of her — this will be remembered of her!"

Jesus to his disciples at a public dinner,

not long before his death, gifting his

woman-friend, Salome, and giving

her thanks

Endnotes

Notes to Chapter 2

1. Gary Chamberlain, "Water's Sacred Meanings," *A Matter of Spirit* (Intercommunity Peace and Justice Center) 82 (Spring 2009): 8.

2. These and other statistics are to be found online, from the United Nations, and at http://www.uscatholic.org/print2156 (5/20/2009) and other sources.

3. Eduardo Galeano, *Mirrors: Stories of Almost Everyone* (New York: Nation Books, 2009), pp. 362, 363.

4. The caste system is technically outlawed/illegal in India, but in reality it still controls most of daily life. It is kept in place by a strange consortium of fundamentalist religions, globalization, and privatization.

5. See Arundhati Roy, *The Checkbook and the Cruise Missile: Conversations with Arundhati Roy*, Interviews by David Barsamian (Cambridge, Mass.: South End Press, 2004), p. 24.

6. Arundhati Roy, *Power Politics*, 2nd ed. (Cambridge, Mass.: South End Press, 2001).

7. Roy, *Power Politics*, pp. 5, 8.

8. Roy, *Power Politics*, p. 24.

9. Roy, *Power Politics*, p. 31.

10. Roy, *Power Politics*, pp. 32-33.

11. Roy, *Power Politics*, p. 25.

12. Roy, quoted in an interview with Amy Goodman, 1 October 2009, found in Jewish Peace News, jpn@jewishpeacenews.net.

Notes to Chapter 3

1. Rabbi Arthur Waskow, 13 November 2008, at the website of the Shalom Center, http://www.theshalomcenter.org.

2. Rabbi Arthur Waskow, 13 November 2008.

3. Rabbi Arthur Waskow, 13 November 2008.

4. Wangari Maathai, quoted 22 April 2005 in "Daily Dig," an online service of the Bruderhof community — unfortunately, no longer available.

5. Krista Tippett, on her public radio program "Speaking of Faith," 30 April 2009.

6. Wangari Maathai, "Fourth 'R' for Earth Day — Reduce, Reuse, Recycle . . . Repair," *Christian Science Monitor,* 22 April 2005, available at http://www.csmonitor .com/2005/0422/p09s01-coop.html.

7. Maathai, "Fourth 'R' for Earth Day."

Notes to Chapter 4

1. See Jeff Dietrich, "Exorcising Jesus," *Catholic Agitator,* a publication of the LA Catholic Worker, 6 June 2008, pp. 1 and 6.

2. "Tanks versus Olive Branches: An Interview with Palestinian Leader Hanan Ashrawi on Feminism, Faith, and the Future of the Palestinian Cause," by Rose Marie Berger, *Sojourners,* February 2005, pp. 22-26.

3. "Tanks versus Olive Branches," p. 24.

4. "Tanks versus Olive Branches," p. 25.

5. For more information, see www.miftah.org.

6. Lynn Gottlieb, *She Who Dwells Within: A Feminist Vision of a Renewed Judaism* (San Francisco: Harper, 1995), p. 193.

7. *Jewish Post:* Your Gateway to the Jewish World, New York. See www.jewish post.com/archives/news/lynn-gottlieb-pioneering-female-rabbi.html.

8. See http://shomershalom.org/blog/2008/12/20.

9. This quotation is from a blog responding to Adam Horowitz's article on Lynn Gottlieb's delegation to Iran.

10. Quoted by Haviv Rettig, *Jerusalem Post,* 29 April 2008.

11. Quoted by Haviv Rettig, *Jerusalem Post,* 29 April 2008.

12. Quoted by Haviv Rettig, *Jerusalem Post,* 29 April 2008.

13. For an account, see http://www.freerepublic.com/focus/f-religion/2008578/posts.

14. See www.thejewishweek.com/viewArticle/c39_a13582/News/international .html.

15. Stuart Jeffries, interview in the "Weekly Review" of the *Guardian Weekly,* 16-22 June 2006, p. 17.

16. Shirin Ebadi, *Iran Awakening: A Memoir of Revolution and Hope* (London: Rider, 2006).

17. Ebadi, *Iran Awakening*, p. 17.
18. Ebadi, *Iran Awakening*, p. 17.
19. Ebadi, *Iran Awakening*, p. 18.
20. Ebadi, *Iran Awakening*, p. 18.

Notes to Chapter 5

1. A smaller version of a barley cake is what the widow of Zarephath of Sidon feeds Elijah when he asks alms of her. She was planning to make her last cake with her last bit of flour and oil, share it with her son, and then wait to die of starvation due to the famine. In response to Elijah's request, she gives him a bit of water and all of the cake, and from that day forth there is enough oil and enough flour, and the three of them — the prophet, the widow, and the child — live on that little bit, shared for more than a year (1 Kings 17:8-16).
2. See "Food Systems in Crisis: Hunger and the Pursuit of Profit," *Development and Peace Newsletter* 33, no. 1 (Fall 2008): 7.
3. From the Declaration of Nyeleni, Mali, 2007, quoted in "Food Systems in Crisis," p. 7.
4. Dorothy Day, *The Long Loneliness* (New York: Harper & Row, 1952).
5. Dan McKanan, interview in the *Catholic Agitator*, April 2008, p. 2.
6. McKanan, interview in the *Catholic Agitator*, April 2008, p. 2.
7. McKanan, interview in the *Catholic Agitator*, April 2008, p. 7.
8. Robert Ellsberg, quoted in a review of *The Duty of Delight: The Diaries of Dorothy Day*, in the *Catholic Agitator*, August 2008, p. 2.
9. This information is taken from the prologue of Roseanne Murphy's *Martyr of the Amazon: The Life of Sister Dorothy Stang* (Maryknoll, N.Y.: Orbis Books, 2007). This is the account that was printed in newspapers, AP reports, and so forth.
10. Quoted in Murphy, *Martyr of the Amazon*, pp. 114-15.
11. Quoted in Murphy, *Martyr of the Amazon*, p. 120.
12. Murphy, *Martyr of the Amazon*, pp. 120-21.
13. Murphy, *Martyr of the Amazon*, p. 122.
14. The following recounting of events draws heavily on Murphy's *Martyr of the Amazon*, pp. 141-55. All subsequent quotations are noted with page numbers in the text.

Notes to Chapter 6

1. "Weekly Review: Marguerite Barankitse, Africa's Answer to Mother Teresa, Talks to Henri Tincq about Her Life's Work," *Guardian Weekly*, April 28–May 4, 2006, p. 17.
2. "Weekly Review: Marguerite Barankitse," p. 17.

3. Interview with Richard Johnson, *The Globe and Mail,* no date.

4. "Maggy's Children," interview with Stephanie Nolen, *The Globe and Mail,* no date.

5. "Maggy's Children," interview with Stephanie Nolen.

6. "Weekly Review: Marguerite Barankitse," p. 17.

7. One version of this story is found in "Reflection" by Tom Clinton-McCausland, *Friends Journal,* June 2007.

8. This interview can be found at http://www.zenit.org/article-23494?1=English, released 28 August 2008.

Notes to Chapter 7

1. *Etty Hillesum: Essential Writings,* selected and with an introduction by Annemarie Kidder, Modern Spiritual Masters Series (Maryknoll, N.Y.: Orbis Books, 2009), pp. 157-58.

2. Quoted by Chris Zimmerman in "A Rare Tribute to the Dead: Kaethe Kollwitz's Memorial to Her Son," found on www.bruderhof.com, 21 November 2005. Unfortunately, this site is no longer available.

3. Quoted by Chris Zimmerman in "A Rare Tribute to the Dead."

4. Eduardo Galeano, *Voices of Time: A Life in Stories,* trans. Mark Fried, Metropolitan Books (New York: Henry Holt & Co., 2006).

5. Galeano, *Voices of Time,* p. 295.

6. Nicole Sotelo, "Not Counting Women and Children," *National Catholic Reporter,* 27 November 2009, p. 20.

7. See *USA Today,* 28 April 2005, and AlterNet.com (www.alternet.com/waroniraq/217999/ from 28 April 2005).

8. Nicole Sotelo, "Not Counting Women and Children," p. 20.

9. Richard Lukas, "Irena Sendler: World War II's Polish Angel," *St. Anthony Messenger,* August 2008, pp. 31-35.

10. Quoted by Richard Lukas in "Irena Sendler."

11. Quoted from the transcripts of the trial held in February 1943.

12. See *Justpeace Pax Christi,* International Catholic Movement for Peace, Newsletter no. 248, May-June 2005, cover page.

13. From *On the Line,* compiled and edited by Mike Wisniewski, Los Angeles Catholic Worker, *The Agitator* 38, no. 2 (April 2008).

14. Joshua McElwee, "Finding Success in Small Steps: Three Iconic Peace Witnesses Speak of Their Struggles, Personal Journeys," *National Catholic Reporter,* 11 December 2009, p. 8.

15. Jody Williams, "*Ingredients for Peace,* A New Cookbook That Offers Recipes from More than Sixty Nobel Peace Prize Laureates and Peace Activists," *USA Today,* quoted in Daily Digest, "Sojourners." See SojoMail@sojo.net, 12 December 2009.

16. Etty Hillesum, *An Interrupted Life* (New York: Picador, 1996).

17. *Etty Hillesum: Essential Writings,* pp. 61-62.

18. Information about Dianna Ortiz in this section comes from Rose Marie Berger and Julie Polter, "Sister Dianna Ortiz: Death's Dance Broken," in *Cloud of Witnesses,* ed. Jim Wallis and Joyce Hollyday, rev. ed. (Maryknoll, N.Y.: Orbis Books, 2005); and Dianna Ortiz, *The Blindfold's Eye: My Journey from Torture to Truth* (Maryknoll, N.Y.: Orbis Books, 2002).

19. "Sister Dianna Ortiz," p. 39.

20. "Sister Dianna Ortiz," p. 41.

21. "Sister Dianna Ortiz," p. 41.

22. "Sister Dianna Ortiz," pp. 41-42.

23. Dianna Ortiz, "A Letter from a Torture Survivor to Those Seeking the Democratic and Republican Nominations for President in 2008," *Tikkun,* January/February 2008, pp. 44-45 (www.tikkun.org).

Notes to Chapter 8

1. Editorial, "Rosa Parks," *Washington Post,* 26 October 2005.

2. Will Haygood, "History Was Ready for Rosa Parks," *Washington Post,* 27 October 2005.

3. Fannie Lou Hamer, quoted in "Stepping Out into Freedom" by Danny Duncan Collum, in *Cloud of Witnesses,* ed. Jim Wallis and Joyce Hollyday, rev. ed. (Maryknoll, N.Y.: Orbis Books, 2005), p. 103.

4. Charles Marsh, *God's Long Summer: Stories of Faith and Civil Rights* (Princeton: Princeton University Press, 1997), pp. 20-22.

5. Quoted in Danny Duncan Collum, "Stepping Out into Freedom," p. 109.

6. See Joyce Hollyday, "Sojourner Truth: Pillar of Fire," in *Cloud of Witnesses,* pp. 118-31, and a chapter from Robert Ellsberg, *Blessed among All Women: Women Saints, Prophets, and Witnesses for Our Time* (New York: Crossroad, 2005).

7. Khalil Abdullah, "At Nearly 80, Si, Dolores Huerta Can," *National Catholic Reporter,* 7 August 2009, p. 11.

8. Most of the information on Digna Ochoa comes from Amnestyusa.org, in a segment on Women Human Rights Champions. See http://women.amnestyusa .org/defenders/dignaochoa.asp.

9. "Happy Birthday, Aung San Suu Kyi," *International Herald Tribune,* 18 June 2005.

10. *The Voice of Hope: Aung San Suu Kyi: Conversations with Alan Clements* (New York: Seven Stories Press, 1997), pp. 164, 175, 228.

11. Eduardo Galeano, *Mirrors: The Story of Almost Everyone,* trans. Mark Fried (New York: Nation Books, 2009), p. 340.

12. This portrait was drawn from Ellen Charles's review of *A Russian Diary: A Journalist's Final Account of Life, Corruption, and Death in Putin's Russia,* in *Mother Jones* online, July 13, 2007.

13. Christiane Amanpour, "Farewell," *New York Times.*

Notes to Chapter 9

1. Isabel Allende, *Paula*, trans. Margaret Sayers Peden (New York: HarperCollins, 1995), pp. 9-10.

2. Jill Briscoe, author, lecturer, and founder of the magazine *Just between Us*, quoted in "Verse of the Day," *Sojourners* online, 4 December 2009.

3. Hildegard of Bingen, *The World of Hildegard of Bingen: Her Life, Times, and Visions*, ed. H. Schipperges, trans. J. Cumming (Collegeville, Minn.: Liturgical Press, 1997), p. 73.

4. Edith Stein, *Essays on Woman*, in *Collected Works of Edith Stein*, vol. 2 (Washington, D.C.: ICS Publications, 1987), p. 84.

5. Margaret Cropper, *Life of Evelyn Underhill* (London: Kessinger Publishing, 1985), p. 225.

6. Timothy Radcliffe, O.P., "St. Catherine of Siena: Patroness of Europe: A Letter to the Dominican Order, Published April 2000, to Celebrate the Naming of Catherine as One of the Patrons of Europe." This can be found on the Web: http://www.op.org/international/english/Documents/masters_order/Radcliffe/Catherine_s 2/5/2006.

7. Radcliffe, "St. Catherine of Siena," p. 2.

8. Catherine of Siena, Letter to Pope Gregory XI (T255), June 1376, in *The Letters of Catherine of Siena*, trans. Suzanne Noffke, vol. 2 (Tempe, Ariz.: Arizona Center for Medieval and Renaissance Texts and Studies, 2001), p. 193.

9. Catherine of Siena, Letter to Pope Gregory XI (T206), March 1376, in *The Letters of Catherine of Siena*, trans. Suzanne Noffke, vol. 1 (Tempe, Ariz.: Arizona Center for Medieval and Renaissance Texts and Studies, 2000), pp. 242-43.

10. Catherine of Siena, Letter to Charles, King of France (T235), August 1376, in *The Letters of Catherine of Siena*, vol. 2, pp. 220-22.

11. Mary Catherine Hilkert, *Speaking with Authority: Catherine of Siena and the Voices of Women Today* (Mahwah, N.J.: Paulist Press, 2008), pp. 121-22.

12. "Terry Tempest Williams," interview in *The Progressive* with David Kupfer, February 2005, pp. 35-40.

13. Williams, interview in *The Progressive*, p. 38.

14. Williams, interview in *The Progressive*, pp. 38-39.

15. Heidi Hart, "A Conversation with Terry Tempest Williams," in *Image: Art, Faith, Mystery*, issue 58, pp. 59-72.

16. Hart, "A Conversation with Terry Tempest Williams," p. 72.

17. Terry Tempest Williams, *Leap* (New York: Pantheon, 2000), p. 265.

18. Ivone Gebara, *Out of the Depths: Women's Experience of Evil and Salvation*, trans. Ann Patrick Ware (Minneapolis: Augsburg Fortress Press, 2002).

19. Gebara, *Out of the Depths*, p. 52.

20. Gebara, *Out of the Depths*, pp. 52-53.

Bibliography

Adler, Frances Payne, Debra Busman, and Diana Garcia, eds. *Fire and Ink: An Anthology of Social Action Writing*. Tucson: University of Arizona Press, 2009.

Allison, Jay, and Dan Gediman, eds., in association with NPR. *This I Believe: The Personal Philosophies of Remarkable Men and Women*. New York: Henry Holt & Co., 2007.

Carter, Anne Laurel. *The Shepherd's Granddaughter*. Toronto: Groundwood Books, House of Anansi Press, 2008.

Cron, Gerald, et al. *Women Also Journey with Him: Feminist Perspectives on the Bible*. Collegeville, Minn.: Liturgical Press, 2000.

Gebara, Ivone. *Longing for Running Water: Ecofeminism and Liberation*. Minneapolis: Fortress Press, 1999.

Gench, Frances Taylor. *Back to the Well: Women's Encounters with Jesus in the Gospels*. Louisville: Westminster John Knox Press, 2004.

Goldstein, Rabbi Elyse, ed. *New Jewish Feminism: Probing the Past, Forging the Future*. Woodstock, Vt.: Jewish Lights Publishing, 2009.

———. *The Woman's Torah Commentary: New Insights from Women Rabbis on the Fifty-four Weekly Torah Portions*. Woodstock, Vt.: Jewish Lights Publishing, 2000.

Gordon, Charlotte. *The Woman Who Named God: Abraham's Dilemma and the Birth of Three Faiths*. New York: Little, Brown & Co., 2009.

Levertov, Denise. *The Stream and the Sapphire: Selected Poems on Religious Themes*. New York: New Directions, 1997.

Nava, Alexander. *The Mystical and Prophetic Thought of Simone Weil and Gustavo Gutiérrez: Reflections on the Mystery and Hiddenness of God.* Albany, N.Y.: State University of New York Press, 2001.

Nitzan, Tal, and Rachel Tzvia Back, eds. *With an Iron Pen: Twenty Years of Hebrew Protest.* Excelsior Editions. Albany, N.Y.: State University of New York Press, 2009.

Orevillo-Montenegro, Muriel. *The Jesus of Asian Women: Women from the Margins.* Maryknoll, N.Y.: Orbis Books, 2006.

Palmer, Martin, and Jay Ramsay, with Man-Ho Kwok. *The Kuan Yin Chronicles: The Myths and Prophecies of the Chinese Goddess of Compassion.* Charlottesville, Va.: Hampton Roads Publishing, 2009.

Rich, Adrienne. *A Human Eye: Essays on Art in Society, 1997-2008.* New York: W. W. Norton & Co., 2009.

————. *Poetry and Commitment.* New York: W. W. Norton & Co., 2007.

Schaefer, Carol. *Grandmothers Counsel the World: Women Elders Offer Their Vision for Our Planet.* Boston: Trumpeter, 2006.

Schireson, Grace. *Zen Women: Beyond the Tea Ladies, Iron Maidens, and Macho Masters.* Boston: Wisdom Publications, 2009.

Sontag, Susan. *Regarding the Pain of Others.* New York: Farrar, Straus & Giroux, 2003.

Tamez, Elsa. *Struggles for Power in Early Christianity.* Maryknoll, N.Y.: Orbis Books, 2007.

Tippett, Krista. *Speaking of Faith.* New York: Viking, 2007.

Williams, Terry Tempest. *Red: Passion and Patience in the Desert.* New York: Pantheon Books, 2001.

Williams, Terry Tempest, and Mary Frank. *Desert Quartet: An Erotic Landscape.* New York: Pantheon Books, 1995.

Women against Wars, Wars against Women. Talks by Arundhati Roy, Nawal el Saddawi, Saher Saba, and Irene Khan. Woods Hole, Mass.: 2 Video Productions, 2006. See www.zmag.org.